# MRCPsych

## PART 2
## PRACTICE PAPERS:
### ISQs AND EMIs

PasTest

to your success

*To my wife*

# MRCPsych

## PART 2
## PRACTICE PAPERS:
## ISQs AND EMIs

### NICHOLAS TAYLOR
MB ChB MRCPsych

Specialist Registrar in Forensic Psychiatry
Reaside Clinic, Birmingham

PasTest
Dedicated to your success

© 2005 PasTest Ltd
Egerton Court
Parkgate Estate
Knutsford
Cheshire, WA16 8DX

Telephone: 01565 752000

First edition 2005

ISBN: 1 904 627 60 9

A catalogue record for this book is available from the British Library.

The information contained within this book was obtained by the author from reliable sources. However, while every effort has been made to ensure its accuracy, no responsibility for loss, damage or injury occasioned to any person acting or refraining from action as a result of information contained herein can be accepted by the publisher or the author.

---

**PasTest Revision Books and Intensive Courses**

PasTest has been established in the field of postgraduate medical education since 1972, providing revision books and intensive study courses for doctors preparing for their professional examinations. Books and courses are available for the following specialties:

MRCP Part 1 and Part 2, MRCPCH Part 1 and Part 2, MRCOG, DRCOG, MRCGP, MRCPsych, DCH, FRCA, MRCS and PLAB.

For further details contact:

**PasTest Ltd, Freepost, Knutsford, Cheshire, WA16 7BR**
Tel: **01565 752000**                   Fax: **01565 650264**
Email: **enquiries@pastest.co.uk**  Web site: **www. pastest.co.uk**

---

Typeset by The Old Tin Dog Design Company, Brighton
Printed and bound by MPG ltd, Bodmin, UK

# CONTENTS

# INTRODUCTION

The sole aim of this book is to help you to prepare for the Part II. It can be used in several ways:

## 1 A guide to the syllabus

The questions follow the syllabus closely and represent the range and depth of knowledge required for the basic sciences and clinical topics parts of the exam. If you can come away from the papers in this book feeling comfortable that you can answer most of them, you probably know enough to pass the ISQs and EMIs in the exam.

## 2 Practice for the exam

The questions are organised into practice papers which follow the format of the exam exactly. The papers are the same length and the questions are equivalent to those in the real exam. Get out the stopwatch, and spent 90 minutes sitting a realistic practice paper. It is important to get the timing right and practice technique by practising complete papers before the real thing.

## 3 A revision textbook

Although this book is no substitute for a comprehensive textbook of psychiatry, the explanations to questions and detailed references will help you to understand the areas which you have not yet revised or which you have difficulty understanding. Flicking through this book for a couple of minutes, or a couple of hours, is an easy and productive way to spend time. The answers are referenced, where relevant, to other textbooks in the PasTest range: *Essential Revision Notes in Psychiatry for MRCPsych* edited by Christopher Fear and *The A-Z of the MRCPsych* by Nicholas Taylor. References are also made to *Symptoms in the Mind, 3rd Edition: An Introduction to Descriptive Psychopathology* by Andrew Sims (Saunders: London, 2003) which you may find useful.

## 4 A guide to your own knowledge

Attempting one of the papers in this book will highlight weaknesses in your own knowledge, and allow you to focus your revision on the areas you need to develop most. Know all about conditioning? Learn about something else instead!

However you choose to use the book; on your own or in a group, at the start of your revision or the day before the exam, I hope it helps you to get the result you deserve.

**Nicholas Taylor**

# EXAMINATION TECHNIQUE

Every candidate has heard all the advice a thousand times. So why do so many people ignore it during one of the most important (and expensive) exams they will ever attempt?

The night before the exam, go to bed and rest (even if you can't sleep) rather than staying up til 3am trying to learn those few "crucial" facts that you think will help you pass the exam. Your ability to learn new material is very poor the night before the exam. Even if you do learn even 30 new facts that night (unlikely), it is almost guaranteed that none of them will be tested in the exam. This will not improve your overall performance. Get some rest, and your cognitive abilities will be better for the whole of the exam. Every question in every paper will benefit from the faster processing speed and improved recall that was restored when you went to bed the night before. This will improve your performance. You will be in the examination venue for at least 6 hours on the day of the exam. If you are exhausted at the start of the day, you just won't make it to the end!

The basic sciences and clinical topics papers consist of 165 individual statement questions (ISQs) and X extended matching items (EMIs), in 90 minutes. The answers to the ISQs are worth one mark each. Negative marking (-1 mark for each incorrect answer) was dropped some years ago, so it makes sense to give an answer to every question, even if it is a guess. Guesses (on average) score 0.5 marks each. The EMIs are arranged into 'themes', with between 3 and 6 questions ('stems') for each theme. Each correct answer to an EMI is worth 3 marks, so this is a very important part of the examination. The total mark is therefore $165 + X = Y$.

In the real exam, you will have lots of adrenaline and very little time. Practice makes perfect. Make yourself practise mock exam papers (like the ones in this book) with a real 90 minute time limit. You will be surprised at how little time you have. You must get used to shifting from subject to subject very quickly, as there are less than 30 seconds for each question.

In your practice exams and in the real exam, go though the paper first, from beginning to end, answering all the questions you feel confident about. Put a small mark next to those you are unsure about, so you can find them easily on your second pass. At the end of the first pass, go through the paper again, looking at the questions you were unsure about. Your unconscious will have been working on them in the meantime, and you will now find you know the answers to some of them – these can be answered quickly. Don't spend too long (certainly more than a minute) thinking about any individual question. You don't have the time and, if you're that unsure, you don't stand a good chance of getting it right anyway. Guess, and use your time more efficiently elsewhere. Towards the end, make sure you have answered every question. If you have no idea about a question, make a guess.

Sleep well, and good luck!

**Nicholas Taylor**

# BASIC SCIENCES
## PRACTICE PAPERS

# PRACTICE PAPER 1

*Time allowed: 90 minutes*

## INDIVIDUAL STATEMENT QUESTIONS

1.1 Piaget described a stage of development known as the formal pre-operational stage.

1.2 Both developmental stages and developmental tasks must be completed in a certain order.

1.3 Slow-wave sleep increases after a longer than usual period of wakefulness.

1.4 All drugs bind plasma.

1.5 The limbic system, formerly known as the Papez circuit, involves the orbitofrontal cortex.

1.6 Drugs with a high relative molecular mass are absorbed more quickly following intravenous administration.

1.7 Risperidone is a benzisoxamole.

1.8 People with schizophrenia cannot become directors of companies.

1.9 Passive diffusion can occur against a concentration gradient.

1.10 Gender is a quantitative variable.

1.11 Consent must be explicit and given in writing if it is to be recognised.

1.12 Selection bias is associated with case–control studies.

1.13 Before screening programmes are established, it is important that there is a reliable surgical treatment available for the disease to be screened for.

**1.14** Consultants should generally dissuade patients from appealing against detention under the Mental Health Act because this interferes with the therapeutic relationship.

**1.15** Specificity is defined as the proportion of people without a given condition who are identified as being disease-free by the test being examined.

**1.16** Standardised mortality rates take into account confounders, most commonly age.

**1.17** Hartnup's disease is autosomal recessive.

**1.18** The 3' end of a gene is downstream.

**1.19** Patau's syndrome has the phenotype 47, +13.

**1.20** The temporal lobe is examined in detail by the Wisconsin card sorting test.

**1.21** The optimal delay in delayed conditioning is 1.5 s.

**1.22** Higher order conditioning is often a factor in the development of simple phobias.

**1.23** There is a link between parent–child discussion and the child's social competency.

**1.24** Figure–ground differentiation applies to both auditory and visual stimuli.

**1.25** The life-style adopted at the age of 20 years usually differs from that adopted by the age of 45 years.

**1.26** Adults with a history of childhood sexual abuse can accurately recall specific times and dates when abuse took place.

**1.27** Elderly people with terminal illness deserve greater care and respect than younger people because they have been of greater benefit to society during their lifetimes.

**1.28** Alcoholism is relatively common in the elderly.

**1.29** Resistance to enculturation helps an individual achieve self-actualisation.

**1.30** Hallucinations are a form of false perception.

**1.31** Allport described both surface and source traits.

**1.32** Canon described homeostasis, which is important in intrinsic theories of motivation.

**1.33** Monozygotic twins have 100% concordance, compared with the 66% concordance between dyzygotic twins.

**1.34** Depressive disorders respond to treatment with placebo.

**1.35** Antidepressant therapy should be discontinued abruptly, to minimise side-effects.

**1.36** In first-order kinetics, the half-life falls with time.

**1.37** Type IV hypersensitivity reactions can present with skin rashes.

**1.38** Fragile X syndrome is the second most common inherited form of mental retardation.

**1.39** Gene probes are made from tiny pieces of metal.

**1.40** Adoption studies are useful because strong intrauterine effects are controlled for.

**1.41** Mitochondrial DNA is passed from mother to daughter and explains the African Eve hypothesis.

**1.42** Down's syndrome is usually caused by non-disjunction during mitosis causing trisomy 21.

**1.43**    Benzodiazepines bind γ-aminobutyric acid A (GABA-A) receptors.

**1.44**    Transcription involves making DNA from RNA.

**1.45**    G-proteins link membrane receptors to a variety of intracellular molecules and responses.

**1.46**    A human with XXXY chromosomes will be phenotypically male.

**1.47**    The clinical effects of typical antipsychotics are mediated by their effects at presynaptic D2 receptors.

**1.48**    Lesch–Nyhan syndrome is a sex-linked disorder.

**1.49**    Acute dystonias tend to occur in the second week of therapy.

**1.50**    Valproate has clinically significant effects on the protein kinase C signalling pathway.

**1.51**    Action potentials are digital signals because they are either on or off, with no mid-point.

**1.52**    Satiety is mediated by the ventrolateral thalamic nucleus.

**1.53**    A lesion in the inferior frontal gyrus is likely to cause difficulties with speech.

**1.54**    Alpha rhythms arise in the frontal lobes and move posteriorly.

**1.55**    Bernouilli distributions are continuous.

**1.56**    Interictal psychosis has a clear relationship to the ictus.

**1.57**    Frontal lobe lesions are associated with apathy.

**1.58**    Confounding factors are related to the exposure and are risk factors for the outcome.

**1.59**    Intelligence is relatively straightforward to define and understand.

**1.60**   The EEG is flattened in Huntington's disease, with complete loss of alpha rhythm.

**1.61**   Positron emission tomography (PET) is most often used in psychiatry to investigate temporal lobe abnormalities.

**1.62**   Drugs can cross the blood–brain barrier by active transport.

**1.63**   The use of lithium was suggested in the 19th century.

**1.64**   Escitalopram is the inactive enantiomer of citalopram.

**1.65**   Reboxetine is a selective serotonin reuptake inhibitor (SSRI).

**1.66**   Noradrenaline is produced from dopamine by dopamine-β-hydroxylase and degraded to tyrosine by catechol-$O$-methyl-transferase (COMT).

**1.67**   Monoamine oxidase A metabolises tyramine and dopamine as its preferred substrates.

**1.68**   A child of 9 years will fail the Sally-Ann-marble test.

**1.69**   Case studies have no value and should not be published.

**1.70**   Validity is improved by increasing sample sizes.

**1.71**   Projective tests have no correct or incorrect answers.

**1.72**   The MRCPsych examination is norm-referenced.

**1.73**   A child with a mentally ill parent can benefit from knowing that their parent's problems are a result of illness and that they are not to blame.

**1.74**   γ-Aminobutyric acid (GABA), synthesised from glutamate, is the main inhibitory neurotransmitter in the brain.

**1.75**   A lesion in the posterior pituitary may lead to a dramatic increase in water intake.

**1.76** The pons contains the trapezoid body.

**1.77** Growth hormone secretion is characteristically reduced as body mass index increases above the normal range.

**1.78** Hypothalamic–hypophyseal portal veins have a central role in the distribution of glutamate within the brain.

**1.79** The hypothalamus is an area of high glutamate concentration.

**1.80** Thyrotropin-releasing hormone from the hypothalamus increases production of thyroid-stimulating hormone in the posterior lobe of the pituitary.

**1.81** The hypothalamus synthesises antidiuretic hormone and oxytocin.

**1.82** Attitudes can be measured using Thurstone's semantic differential scale, which is a seven-point scale.

**1.83** All maternal illnesses affecting birth weight lead to microsomia.

**1.84** Tardive dyskinesia is caused by changes in dopamine receptor expression in the cerebellum.

**1.85** Theta rhythms are increased by antipsychotics.

**1.86** Selective serotonin reuptake inhibitor (SSRI) discontinuation syndromes are reduced after discontinuation of an SSRI with a long half-life.

**1.87** Goffman referred to total institutions as the only places which could offer totally therapeutic environments.

**1.88** According to Brown and Harris, a woman with no confiding relationship is at elevated risk of suffering a depressive disorder.

**1.89** Children are not influenced by the media.

**1.90** A test dose of a new drug is useful in excluding hypersensitivity. A second dose can then be given with confidence.

**1.91** Advanced neuroimaging techniques can accurately measure receptor occupancy in the human brain.

**1.92** D5 receptors are similar to D1 receptors.

**1.93** The placebo effect is most pronounced with tablets of average size.

**1.94** No significantly new classes of psychotropic drugs have been introduced since the late 1970s.

**1.95** Tuberous sclerosis characteristically causes tubers in the sulci.

**1.96** Efferents from the locus caeruleus are widespread.

**1.97** Action potentials are characterised by calcium influx.

**1.98** Drugs are commonly excreted by the liver.

**1.99** Active transport occurs across the blood–brain barrier, allowing drugs to move against a concentration gradient.

**1.100** Dopamine is synthesised from dihydroxyphenylalanine (DOPA), which is synthesised from tyrosine.

**1.101** Satiety is mediated by the ventromedial hypothalamic nucleus.

**1.102** A flat trace on a properly conducted EEG is an unequivocal sign of brain death.

**1.103** Giraffe bodies are characteristic of Hurler's disease.

**1.104** Gadolinium is used as a contrast enhancer in magnetic resonance imaging.

**1.105** Case–control studies involve a group of cases and a group of controls. The two groups differ because one has been selected by the designers of the study and one has been selected at random.

**1.106** Culture is partially determined by physical objects.

**1.107** Durkheim suggested that high social integration is protective against suicide.

**1.108** There is currently a major shift from community-based care to inpatient care in the management of the severely mentally unwell.

**1.109** Epilepsy is associated with lissencephaly, which is the development of abnormally prominent gyri and sulci within the brain.

**1.110** In receptive dysphasia, the ability to repeat messages is preserved.

**1.111** In schizophrenia, there is a relative excess of glutamate and aspartate, with a relative lack of serotonin.

**1.112** The medial temporal lobe is normal in schizophrenia.

**1.113** Life events can be positive or negative.

**1.114** Insecure attachment is associated with emotional disorders occurring later in childhood and subsequent disorders in adulthood.

**1.115** Cortical dementia commonly involves subcortical neurones.

**1.116** Infant temperament may have a powerful effect on the parent–child relationship.

**1.117** Stigma develops during the stage of industry versus inferiority.

**1.118** Few 4-year-old children have any fears.

**1.119** Obstetric complications can lead to the development of physical but not psychiatric illnesses.

**1.120** Aggression can be defined as instrumental or hostile/instructive.

**1.121** When an autocratic leader is absent from the group, constructive work most often continues.

**1.122** Children raised by homosexual partners acting as parents go on to develop gender identity disorder.

**1.123** Exposure to adversity has an effect on mental health by reducing the average age of onset of schizophrenia.

**1.124** Illness always has a physical cause.

**1.125** Urbanisation is good because it prevents people from becoming isolated.

**1.126** Dysphasia and paragrammatism can lead to speech which cannot be understood.

**1.127** Inferential statistics involve the measurement of whole populations to draw more accurate conclusions.

**1.128** Survival curves are often depicted as a series of discrete steps, rather than as true curves.

**1.129** Weber placed a greater emphasis than Marx on economic factors in maintaining class boundaries.

**1.130** Marital schism, described by Lidz, occurs when there is a power struggle between a parent and a child.

**1.131** Doctors contribute to a patient's role in being sick by legitimising their illness.

**1.132** Fusion is identified with a weak determining tendency.

**1.133** Lesions in the occipital lobe characteristically cause astereognosia.

**1.134** Depersonalisation is experienced as a disorder of self.

**1.135**   Anhedonia is defined as loss of the capacity to experience emotion.

**1.136**   Opalski cells are characteristic of Tay–Sachs disease.

**1.137**   When using computed tomography, cerebral infarcts are best detected very soon after they occur.

**1.138**   The winter excess of births of children going on to develop schizophrenia is most marked in families with a history of schizophrenia.

**1.139**   Lesions of the anterior hypothalamus preserve sexual activity.

**1.140**   Conative dissonance was described by Festinger.

**1.141**   Symptoms of multiple sclerosis include paralysis, vertigo and dilated pupils.

**1.142**   The anterior commissure is part of the lamina terminalis.

**1.143**   Hallucinations can only occur in one modality at any given time.

**1.144**   The heritability of austism is 0.90.

**1.145**   Psychodynamic family therapy investigates conscious rather than unconscious factors.

**1.146**   The medical model of psychiatry suggests that it is a fact that there is something wrong with the individual's mental state.

**1.147**   Langfeldt described process schizophrenia.

**1.148**   Foucault wrote *The Birth of the Clinic* and portrayed madness as a social construction.

**1.149**   Cross-over designs involve two groups undergoing tests in different orders.

**1.150**   Telegraphic speech involves the use of nouns at the expense of verbs.

**1.151** The fasciculus gracilis is an ascending tract in the spinal cord.

**1.152** Generalised anxiety disorder involves septohippocampal difficulties with anxiety mediation.

**1.153** The prohibition paradox suggests that litigation helps to prevent crime by prohibiting it.

**1.154** Emotional tone may be appropriate in emotional lability.

**1.155** Pore filtration occurs across the wall of the small intestine but not the stomach.

**1.156** Secondary prevention involves work on relapse to prevent a relapse in a patient who has suffered one episode of a disease.

**1.157** Delirium can result from trauma or hypoxia.

**1.158** Survival analysis can be used to compare two populations and uses Cox's proportional hazards regression analysis if more than one variable is to be compared.

**1.159** Tanycytes line the floor of the fourth ventricle.

**1.160** Handling is seen in catatonic schizophrenia.

**1.161** Pharmacogenetics involves modifying disease genes to benefit the patient.

**1.162** In certain circumstances, treatment can be given to a patient who does not consent.

**1.163** It has been suggested that women become depressed more often than men because they are more prone to rumination.

**1.164** The superego often acts as a conscience.

**1.165** Almost a third of people over 90 years old have dementia.

# EXTENDED MATCHING ITEMS

## 1.166 THEME: EEG PHENOMENA

| | |
|---|---|
| A | Alpha rhythms |
| B | Beta rhythms |
| C | Delta rhythms |
| D | Flat trace |
| E | Intermittent generalised seizure activity |
| F | Lambda rhythms |
| G | Mu rhythms |
| H | Spikes |
| I | Theta rhythms |
| J | Waves |

**For each of the following descriptions, identify the EEG phenomenon from the list above**

1    Occur when awake, alert and paying attention.
2    Seen in occipital regions with the eyes open.
3    Frequency less than 4 Hz.

## 1.167   THEME: EFFECTS OF MEDICATION

| | |
|---|---|
| A | Ataxia |
| B | Dependence |
| C | Diabetes mellitus |
| D | Increase in the seizure threshold |
| E | Leucopenia |
| F | Neuroleptic malignant syndrome |
| G | Pigmentation |
| H | Reduction in the seizure threshold |
| I | Tiredness the following morning |
| J | Weight loss |

**For each of the following medications, choose the most common effect from the list above.**

| | |
|---|---|
| 1 | Chlorpromazine |
| 2 | Semisodium valproate |
| 3 | Zopiclone. |

## 1.168    THEME: CONDITIONING

| | |
|---|---|
| A | Conditioned discrimination |
| B | Continuous reinforcement |
| C | Fixed interval reinforcement |
| D | Higher order conditioning |
| E | Learned helplessness |
| F | Negative reinforcement |
| G | Punishment |
| H | Stimulus generalisation |
| I | Stimulus preparedness |
| J | Variable ratio reinforcement |

**Choose the most appropriate term from the list above to describe each of the following:**

1    An aversive stimulus is presented shortly after a behaviour is performed.

2    An aversive stimulus which, although present initially, can be removed by certain behaviours.

3    Every conditioned response leads to reinforcement.

## 1.169   THEME: NAMES AND IDEAS

| | |
|---|---|
| A | Arthur Janov |
| B | Carl Schneider |
| C | Ernest Kretschmer |
| D | James |
| E | Kurt Schneider |
| F | Lidz |
| G | Melanie Klein |
| H | Seligman |
| I | Winnicott |
| J | Sigmund Freud |

**Choose the name from the above list most closely associated with each of the following ideas:**

1   Learned helplessness
2   Primal therapy
3   Derailment.

## 1.170   THEME: SIDE-EFFECTS OF ANTIPSYCHOTIC MEDICATION

| | |
|---|---|
| A | The arcuate fasciculus |
| B | The cerebral peduncle |
| C | The corpus callosum |
| D | The corticospinal tract |
| E | The limbic system |
| F | The mesolimbic–mesocortical pathway |
| G | The nigrostriatal tract |
| H | The pyramidal tract |
| I | The stria terminalis |
| J | The tuberoinfundibular pathway |

Choose the area from the list above which is most involved in each of the following effects:

1   Hyperprolactinaemia caused by haloperidol.
2   Extrapyramidal side-effects caused by trifluoperazine.
3   Akathisia caused by phenothiazines.

## 1.171   THEME: RECEPTOR-MEDIATED SIDE-EFFECTS

| | |
|---|---|
| A | $\alpha_1$-Adrenergic receptors |
| B | Central muscarinic acetylcholinergic receptors |
| C | D2 receptors in the mesolimbic–mesocortical pathway |
| D | D2 receptors in the nigrostriatal pathway |
| E | D2 receptors in the tuberoinfundibular pathway |
| F | D3 receptors |
| G | D4 receptors |
| H | Histamine receptors |
| I | NMDA receptor |
| J | Peripheral muscarinic acetylcholinergic receptors |

**For each of the following effects, choose the receptor which mediates it from the list above:**

1   Convulsions and pyrexia caused by tricyclic antidepressants.
2   Hyperprolactinaemia caused by antipsychotics.
3   Ejaculatory failure caused by typical antipsychotics.
4   Urinary retention and constipation caused by tricyclic antidepressants.

## 1.172 THEME: STATISTICS

| | |
|---|---|
| A | Absolute risk increase (ARI) |
| B | Control event rate (CER) |
| C | Number needed to harm (NNH) |
| D | Number needed to treat (NNT) |
| E | Positive predictive value (PPV) |
| F | Post-test odds |
| G | Relative risk reduction (RRR) |
| H | Sensitivity |
| I | Sensitivity/(1 – Specificity) |
| J | Specificity |

**Choose the term from the list above which equates to each of the following:**

1   Risk of outcome event in the control group.
2   EER-CER.
3   Proportion of test positives with the target disorder.
4   Likelihood ratio for a positive result (LR +).
5   Proportion of true negatives correctly identified.

## 1.173   THEME: RELIABILITY AND VALIDITY

| | |
|---|---|
| A | Concurrent validity |
| B | Construct validity |
| C | External validity |
| D | Face validity |
| E | Incremental validity |
| F | Inter-rater reliability |
| G | Parallel (alternative) form reliability |
| H | Predictive validity |
| I | Split-half reliability |
| J | Test–retest reliability |

**Choose the most appropriate term from the list above for each of the following:**

1      The consistency of a measure from one time to another.
2      The extent to which similar questions correlate.
3      The extent to which it is appropriate to apply results to other populations.
4      The level of consistency of two tests constructed in the same way from the same content domain.
5      The consistency between two halves of the same test.

# PRACTICE PAPER 1

## Answers

### INDIVIDUAL STATEMENT QUESTIONS

1.1     **False** – He described the pre-operational stage and the formal operational stage.
A–Z p253–5

1.2     **False** – The child must progress through developmental stages (as seen in the theories of Erikson, Freud and Piaget) sequentially, but developmental task theory states that developmental tasks (such as learning to take solid food, to crawl, to talk, etc) can be completed at different rates and that children will achieve them in different orders.

1.3     **True**

1.4     **True**
A–Z p120–2

1.5     **True**
Fear p116

1.6     **False** – Insoluble drugs cannot be given intravenously.

1.7     **True**

1.8     **False**

1.9     **False**

1.10    **False** – It is qualitative. Quantitative variables can be measured on a scale and compared.

1.11    **False** – Consent can be implied and is often given verbally.

1.12    **True**

Fear p212

1.13    **False** – There should be a safe, reliable, affordable treatment, but it does not have to be surgical.

1.14    **False**

1.15    **True**

1.16    **True**

1.17    **True**

1.18    **True**

1.19    **False** – This is the genotype.

1.20    **False** – This test tests frontal lobe function.
A–Z p351

1.21    **False** – The optimal delay is approximately 0.5 s.

1.22    **False** – Higher order conditioning occurs when a new conditioned stimulus develops as a result of pairing of an established conditioned stimulus with a neutral stimulus.

1.23    **True** – Children of authoritarian parents, who do not discuss matters with their children, generally have poorer social competence than children of authoritative parents, who welcome discussion with their children.

1.24    **True** – In the visual sense, it explains why shapes stand out from the background. In auditory terms, it explains 'the cocktail party effect', when your attention is distracted from the immediate conversation by someone mentioning your name behind you.

1.25    **True**

1.26    **False** – Whilst this may be the case, it cannot be relied upon and many children will remember relatively little, depending on their age and maturity at the time of the abuse.

PAPER I
ANSWERS

**1.27**   **False** – All patients deserve the same level of care and respect.

**1.28**   **True** – Although the elderly form only a small proportion of patients attending specialist drug and alcohol services, alcohol-related problems in the elderly account for large numbers of hospital admissions.

**1.29**   **True** – Detachment and a democratic philosophy are also helpful.

**1.30**   **True** – False perceptions include illusions, hallucinations and pseudohallucinations.
Sims p96–111

**1.31**   **False** – Allport described cardinal, central and secondary traits. Cattel described surface and source traits.
Fear p17

**1.32**   **False** – Canon did describe homeostasis, but this relates to extrinsic theories, which explain motivation in terms of reducing the level of arousal relating to basic drives such as hunger and thirst.
A–Z p217

**1.33**   **False** – Dizygotic twins have 50% concordance.

**1.34**   **True** – For examination purposes, everything responds to placebo.

**1.35**   **False** – Discontinuation should be gradual, to minimise discontinuation effects.

**1.36**   **False** – This is not necessarily the case but can be seen when enzymes are induced by the drug.
Fear p145

**1.37**   **True** – Or they can present with generalised damage resembling systemic lupus erythematosus.

**1.38**  **False** – It is the most common.

**1.39**  **False** – They are made from DNA which complements the DNA under examination.

**1.40**  **False** – Strong intrauterine effects are confounders and are not possible to control for.

**1.41**  **True**

**1.42**  **False** – The non-disjunction occurs during meiosis.

**1.43**  **True**

**1.44**  **False** – It involves making RNA from DNA.

**1.45**  **True**

**1.46**  **True**

**1.47**  **False** – The effects are mediated by postsynaptic D2 receptors.

**1.48**  **True** – It has an X-linked recessive inheritance pattern. See Fear p186–7 for an overview of important inherited conditions and their inheritance patterns.

**1.49**  **False** – They almost invariably occur in the first week.

**1.50**  **True**

**1.51**  **True** – The neuronal membrane either depolarises and transmits an action potential, or it does not. There is no scope for fractions of action potentials.

**1.52**  **False** – Satiety is mediated by the ventromedial nucleus.

**1.53**  **True** – This is the location of Broca's area.

**1.54**  **False** – They arise in the occipital lobes.

1.55 **False** – They are discrete and have only two possible variables, 0 and 1.

1.56 **False**
Fear p325

1.57 **True**

1.58 **True** – The most frequently encountered confounder is age.

1.59 **False** – It is a complex construct with many different aspects, which is generally poorly defined.

1.60 **True**
A–Z p 365–6

1.61 **False** – It is a research tool.

1.62 **True** – Such as levodopa.
A–Z p120–2

1.63 **True** – By Lange in 1886.

1.64 **False** – It is the active enantiomer. An enantiomer is an isomer.

1.65 **False** – It is a selective noradrenaline reuptake inhibitor.

1.66 **False** – It is degraded to methylhydroxyphenylglycol (MHPG), as well as other compounds.
A–Z p226, Fear p154

1.67 **False** – Serotonin and noradrenaline are the preferred substrates for monoamine oxidase A (MAO-A). Dopamine is the preferred substrate for MAO-B.
A–Z p212–13, Fear p157

1.68 **False** – This tests for theory of mind, which is acquired by 4–5 years.
A–Z p319

**1.69** **False** – They have little statistical value and are published less often than other studies, but can be of use.

**1.70** **True** – Validity is a measure of the likelihood that a finding does not result from chance.

**1.71** **True** – They include subjective judgements about responses to ambiguous stimuli.

**1.72** **False** – According to the Royal College, the MRCPsych is criterion-referenced.

**1.73** **True**

**1.74** **True**
Fear p153

**1.75** **True** – It can cause diabetes insipidus, by reducing antidiuretic hormone. This causes a marked diuretic effect.

**1.76** **True**
A–Z p258

**1.77** **True**

**1.78** **False** – They have an important function in the neuroendocrine system but not in neurotransmission.

**1.79** **False** – It is high in serotonergic neurones.

**1.80** **False** – It is the anterior lobe which produces thyroid-stimulating hormone.

**1.81** **True** – These are synthesised in the hypothalamus and secreted by the posterior lobe of the pituitary.

**1.82** **False** – Osgood described a seven-point semantic differential scale. Thurstone used an 11-point scale.
A–Z p50, Fear p27–8

**1.83** **False** – Although many maternal disorders cause microsomia, maternal diabetes is the most common cause of macrosomia, which is seen in up to 10% of births.

1.84  **False** – In the basal ganglia.

1.85  **True**
A–Z p366

1.86  **True**

1.87  **False** – Goffman identified the deficiencies in the institutions and regarded them as anti-therapeutic.

1.88  **True**

1.89  **False** – Children are influenced by the media in many ways. There is a correlation between boys' exposure to televised violence and violent behaviour.
A–Z p204–5

1.90  **False** – The first dose may induce hypersensitivity, which may only be clinically apparent with the second dose.

1.91  **True**

1.92  **True**
Fear p155

1.93  **False** – Very large or very small tablets are more powerful placebos.

1.94  **False** – The 1980s saw the introduction of selective serotonin reuptake inhibitors (SSRIs), amongst others.

1.95  **False** – The tubers occur in the gyri.

1.96  **True** – Suggesting that it has many different functions.

1.97  **True**

1.98  **False** – They are metabolised by the liver, but generally excreted by the kidneys.

**1.99** **True**

**1.100** **True**

**1.101** **True** – Thirst and hunger are mediated by the lateral hypothalamus.

**1.102** **False** – It can indicate brain death or hypothermia. The most common cause of a flat trace in clinical practice is failure to connect the leads properly.

**1.103** **False** – Zebra bodies are seen in Hurler's disease. They are caused by accumulation of storage material in the lysosomes, which swell and appear striped.

**1.104** **True**

**1.105** **False** – The groups differ because one group (the cases) has the disease under study.

**1.106** **True** – Culture is composed of values, norms, principles and material goods.
A–Z p88, Fear p79

**1.107** **True**

**1.108** **False**

**1.109** **False** – Epilepsy is associated with lissencephaly, which is an unusually smooth brain, with reduced gyri and sulci.

**1.110** **False**
A–Z p128

**1.111** **False** – The reverse is true.

**1.112** **False** – There are characteristically changes in this area, although the significance of these is unclear.
A–Z p284, Fear p225

**1.113**  **True** – Psychological and psychiatric problems are associated with both types because any significant change can be difficult to deal with.

**1.114**  **True** – These include school refusal, agoraphobia and others. A–Z p306–7

**1.115**  **True** A–Z p97

**1.116**  **True** – Infants with temperaments causing them to be easy to care for may enjoy better parent–child relationships.

**1.117**  **True** – This is when cultural knowledge is acquired and children become acutely aware of the way in which they are viewed by the world.

**1.118**  **False** – Common fears at this age include loud noises, darkness, animals and monsters. A–Z p144–5

**1.119**  **False** – There are strong associations between perinatal injury and later neurodegenerative disorders, including schizophrenia.

**1.120**  **False** – Aggression can be categorised as instrumental, where there is an identifiable material gain, and hostile/affective, where the aim is simply to cause harm to others.

**1.121**  **False** – The absence of an autocratic leader usually leads to chaos, disruption and abandonment of the task. A–Z p192

**1.122**  **False** – There is no correlation between homosexual parent figures and mental disorder.

**1.123**  **True**

**1.124**  **False** – The causes of illness can be mental or social.

**1.125**  **False** – This statement is too general. Many people are isolated in the urban environment despite living in close proximity to many others.

**1.126** **True**
Sims p175

**1.127** **False** – They measure samples and make inferences about the whole population.

**1.128** **True**

**1.129** **False** – Economic factors were central to Marxist theory. Weber identified other factors as important in maintaining divisions in society, including property, prestige and power.

**1.130** **False** – This is marital skew. Marital schism occurs when one child becomes over-involved with a child of the opposite sex.

**1.131** **True** – This was fundamental to Parsons' concept of the sick role.
Fear p88

**1.132** **True** – Fusion is the illogical linking of two or more unrelated thoughts and is associated with a weak determining tendency, which occurs when there is little overall direction to a person's thinking.

**1.133** **False** – They cause pseudoagnosia. Lesions in the parietal lobe cause astereognosia.

**1.134** **True** – It results from a change in the way the self is experienced.
Sims p214

**1.135** **False** – It is the inability to experience pleasure.

**1.136** **False** – They are characteristic of Wilson's disease.

**1.137** **False** – They are often undetectable for the first 24 hours on computed tomography.

**1.138** **False** – It is more prominent in families with no history.

**1.139**   **True**

**1.140**   **False** – Festinger described cognitive dissonance. There is a conative, or behavioural, component of attitude.

**1.141**   **False** – Not dilated pupils.
Fear p325

**1.142**   **True**
Fear p124

**1.143**   **False** – They can occur in several modalities at the same time, as in severe depressive disorders with concurrent olfactory and visual hallucinations.

**1.144**   **True**
Fear p187

**1.145**   **False** – It investigates both.
Fear p521

**1.146**   **True**
Fear p556

**1.147**   **True**

**1.148**   **True**

**1.149**   **True**
Fear p73

**1.150**   **False** – It involves the use of both.
Fear p49

**1.151**   **True**
Fear p135

**1.152**   **True**
Fear p243

**1.153**   **False** – It does not prevent crime.

Fear p283

**1.154** **True** – Although the tone may be appropriate, it may be excessive and fluctuating.

**1.155** **False** – It occurs in both.

**1.156** **False** – That describes tertiary prevention. Secondary prevention helps the patient after symptoms of an episode have started to present.

**1.157** **True**

**1.158** **True**

**1.159** **False** – They line the floor of the third ventricle.

**1.160** **True** – This is excessive touching of objects.
Fear p97

**1.161** **False** – It involves tailoring drug treatment to take advantage of an individual's genetic pattern.

**1.162** **True**

**1.163** **True** – This is the response style theory.
Fear p235

**1.164** **True**

**1.165** **True**

# EXTENDED MATCHING ITEMS

## 1.166  THEME: EEG PHENOMENA

1    **B** – Beta rhythms
2    **F** – Lambda rhythms
3    **C** – Delta rhythms.

## 1.167  THEME: EFFECTS OF MEDICATION

1    **H** – Reduction in the seizure threshold
2    **D** – Increase in the seizure threshold
3    **I** – Tiredness the following morning.

## 1.168  THEME: CONDITIONING

1    **G** – Punishment
2    **F** – Negative reinforcement
3    **B** – Continuous reinforcement.

## 1.169  THEME: NAMES AND IDEAS

1    **H** – Seligman
2    **A** – Arthur Janov
3    **B** – Carl Schneider.

## 1.170  THEME: SIDE-EFFECTS OF ANTIPSYCHOTIC MEDICATION

1    **J** – The tuberoinfundibular pathway
2    **G** – The nigrostriatal tract
3    **F**– The mesolimbic–mesocortical pathway.
A–Z p34–8

## 1.171  THEME: RECEPTOR-MEDIATED SIDE-EFFECTS

1    **B** – Central muscarinic acetylcholinergic receptors
2    **E** – D2 receptors in the tuberoinfundibular pathway
3    **A** – $\alpha_1$-Adrenergic receptors
4    **J** – Peripheral muscarinic acetylcholinergic receptors.
A–Z p31–8

## 1.172 THEME: STATISTICS

1    **B** – Control event rate (CER)
2    **A** – Absolute risk increase (ARI)
3    **E** – Positive predictive value (PPV)
4    **I** – Sensitivity/(1 – Specificity)
5    **J** – Specificity.
Fear p346–7

## 1.173 THEME: RELIABILITY AND VALIDITY

1    **J** – Test–retest reliability
2    **B** – Construct validity
3    **C** – External validity
4    **G** – Parallel (alternative) form reliability
5    **I** – Split-half reliability.

# PRACTICE PAPER 2

*Time allowed: 90 minutes*

## INDIVIDUAL STATEMENT QUESTIONS

**2.1** Only moderate to heavy drinking in pregnancy can cause harm to the fetus.

**2.2** The parent's phenotype is important in determining quality of parenting. The child's phenotype is of no consequence.

**2.3** Age is a commonly encountered confounding variable.

**2.4** The more restrictive the detention of a patient, the more important the process of appeal becomes.

**2.5** Hypersecretion of growth hormone in children can cause gigantism, whereas in adults it has few significant clinical effects.

**2.6** The positive predictive value of a test is determined entirely by the sensitivity and specificity of the test.

**2.7** Randomised controlled trials should report the 'number needed to treat'.

**2.8** Advocates have rights enshrined in law.

**2.9** In a large group setting there is an emphasis on sociocultural learning.

**2.10** Placebo medication should be given to patients who somatise as this will alleviate their anxiety and avoid side-effects.

**2.11** The neurochemical effects of electroconvulsive therapy are limited to noradrenaline and $\gamma$-aminobutyric acid (GABA).

**2.12** Point prevalence is synonymous with incidence.

**2.13** The problem of selection bias is particularly great with cohort studies.

**2.14** Expressed emotion can be measured by the Camberwell Family Interview.

**2.15** Bipolar disorder has a negative correlation with social class.

**2.16** Goffman included both monasteries and small ships as examples of total institutions.

**2.17** Irish populations in the United Kingdom have higher rates of schizophrenia than South Asian populations.

**2.18** According to Brown and Harris, a woman who lost her mother before the age of 12 is at risk of depression, even if she did not have a good relationship with her mother.

**2.19** Ecological studies are largely free from confounding factors.

**2.20** The telophase II stage in the cell cycle is seen in somatic cells but not in the production of gametes.

**2.21** Phenylketonuria is associated with increased signal from cerebral white matter on magnetic resonance imaging.

**2.22** Dominant parietal lobe lesions cause Gerstmann's syndrome.

**2.23** Witzelsucht is characteristic of frontal lobe damage.

**2.24** EEG spikes are exaggerated in Huntington's disease.

**2.25** Within DNA, guanine complements cytokines.

**2.26** Most inborn errors of metabolism are autosomal dominant.

**2.27** Family studies can differentiate reliably between effects due to nature and effects due to nurture.

**2.28**   Some genes are protective against psychiatric disorders.

**2.29**   LOD scores are used to measure levels of mutation.

**2.30**   The blood–brain barrier is selectively permeable.

**2.31**   Haloperidol is a piperazine compound and is therefore a potent antipsychotic with a marked tendency towards extrapyramidal side-effects.

**2.32**   Insoluble drugs are best given intravenously, as this increases absorption.

**2.33**   Investigation of a suspected lesion in the cerebellum is best performed with computed tomography.

**2.34**   The limbic system contains all of the hypothalamus except the mamillary bodies.

**2.35**   Widening of sulci is seen in Alzheimer's disease.

**2.36**   Overall brain volume is reduced in schizophrenia, in men and women.

**2.37**   Restriction fragment length polymorphisms can be used as DNA markers.

**2.38**   Hyperprolactinaemia can reduce the sperm count in healthy males.

**2.39**   In X-linked recessive conditions, the father is usually the carrier.

**2.40**   Lorenz was an ethologist.

**2.41**   As well as its effects on growth, growth hormone influences glucose levels.

**2.42**   Dopamine reduces prolactin production in the anterior lobe of the pituitary.

**2.43**   The preoptic nucleus of the hypothalamus secretes gonadotrophin-releasing hormone.

**2.44**   The limbic system has an important role in the level of anxiety.

**2.45**   Verbal short-term memory is localised to the left (dominant) hemisphere.

**2.46**   Rett's syndrome is an X-linked dominant disorder.

**2.47**   The heritability of schizophrenia is 0.2.

**2.48**   There are approximately 100,000 genes in humans.

**2.49**   Olanzapine is a quinolinone.

**2.50**   Fluoxetine, fluvoxamine and escitalopram are all selective serotonin reuptake inhibitors.

**2.51**   Opioid receptors include $\mu$-receptors, which mediate dysphoria.

**2.52**   Frontal lobe damage can lead to marked inflexibility.

**2.53**   Noradrenaline, dopamine and serotonin are catecholamines, which are a subgroup of monoamines.

**2.54**   Fragile X syndrome involves multiple CAG repeats.

**2.55**   The major target for the second messenger cAMP is protein kinase A.

**2.56**   Tranylcypromine has an amphetamine-like structure.

**2.57**   Drugs inhibiting $\gamma$-aminobutyric acid (GABA) transaminase act as anticonvulsants.

**2.58**   It is important to monitor blood levels of typical antipsychotics, because of the danger of overdosage.

**2.59**   D4 receptors are found in high concentrations in the frontal lobe.

**2.60** Chelation can result from interactions between drugs.

**2.61** Idiosyncratic drug reactions are most often explained in terms of malingering.

**2.62** Secondary messenger systems have no influence on gene expression.

**2.63** G-proteins consist of three subunits.

**2.64** The antihistaminergic action of typical antipsychotics results in ejaculatory failure.

**2.65** Plasma protein binding is non-competitive and reversible.

**2.66** The γ-aminobutyric acid B (GABA-B) receptor is an ion channel.

**2.67** Neurofibrillary tangles are a normal feature in the ageing brain.

**2.68** The short-term life expectancy of a suddenly-bereaved elderly person is significantly reduced.

**2.69** Elderly people who are free from psychological problems tend not to reminisce because they are living for the present.

**2.70** The pathological process in Parkinson's disease leads to a reactive astrocytosis.

**2.71** Autism is strongly associated with macrocephaly.

**2.72** In schizophrenia, the corpus callosum may be hypertrophic, but is never atrophic.

**2.73** Lewy bodies are found in great abundance in dead neuronal tissue in Parkinson's disease.

**2.74** D4 receptors are similar to D1 receptors.

**2.75** The half-life of a drug with first-order kinetics is generally less than that of a drug with zero-order kinetics.

**2.76** Cage was influential in the early development of lithium for clinical use.

**2.77** Reserpine has been used clinically as a treatment for depressive disorders.

**2.78** Following a day spent resting, slow-wave sleep increases.

**2.79** Posterior column damage causes loss of vibration sense.

**2.80** Lack of sleep reduces growth hormone secretion.

**2.81** Fetal alcohol syndrome causes liver damage in the child, cleft lip and cleft palate.

**2.82** A lesion in the left angular gyrus can cause finger agnosia and spelling errors.

**2.83** It has been suggested that a variety of factors including exposure to viruses and cold temperatures, particularly in the first trimester of pregnancy, can lead to neurodevelopmental disorders in adults.

**2.84** It has been suggested that prenatal exposure to severe maternal nutritional deficiency in early pregnancy can lead to personality disorder.

**2.85** The slow-to-warm-up child shows mildly negative responses to new situations which are psychologically rooted.

**2.86** EEG waves have a duration of 50–80 ms.

**2.87** Enzyme deficiency in the newborn can cause genotype–phenotype differences.

**2.88** Difficulties with syntax may follow a lesion in the front of the dominant cerebral hemisphere.

**2.89** Beta rhythms have a frequency of 13–30 Hz.

**2.90**  The two stages of separation anxiety are 'protest' and 'despair'.

**2.91**  The same actions, carried out on different occasions, can be labelled as primary deviance on one occasion and secondary deviance on another.

**2.92**  People can become desensitised to violence when it is shown on television.

**2.93**  Social class is static and does not change over time.

**2.94**  Psychiatrists have been prominent anti-psychiatrists.

**2.95**  Parenting tasks change over time.

**2.96**  Older people often have fewer social contacts than younger people.

**2.97**  Crisis and turmoil are so common in adolescence that absence of these during adolescence is pathological.

**2.98**  Short-term memory declines with age.

**2.99**  The relative refractory period follows the absolute refractory period.

**2.100**  Broca's area is also known as the sensory speech and language area.

**2.101**  Melatonin is secreted maximally during the early afternoon, by the pineal gland.

**2.102**  Dopamine is broken down to homovanillic acid (HVA) and dihydroxyphenylacetic acid (DOPAC).

**2.103**  Magnetic resonance imaging is a voxel-based imaging technique.

**2.104**  Neurones within the locus caeruleus are important in regulation of the diurnal rhythm.

**2.105** Alpha rhythms are seen on the EEG when the eyes are closed.

**2.106** Episodic memory is a subtype of declarative memory.

**2.107** Alogia is the outward manifestation of poverty of thought.

**2.108** Cerebrospinal fluid flows from the lateral ventricles, through the intraventricular foramina of Munro, to the third ventricle.

**2.109** Lewy bodies in the temporal cortex are suggestive of Parkinson's disease.

**2.110** Frankl described existential legotherapy.

**2.111** For women, being married is a risk factor which increases the incidence of mental illness.

**2.112** The distinction between health and illness is clear and can be made with confidence.

**2.113** Evidence suggests a link between early and prolonged exposure to an urban environment and the subsequent development of schizophrenia.

**2.114** Goffman's total institution involves a clear distinction between patients and staff.

**2.115** Reciprocal inhibition, used to treat phobias, was described by Wolfe.

**2.116** During inattention, affect illusions and pareidolic illusions are more likely than completion illusions.

**2.117** Concepts feature salient attributes which increase perceptual efficiency by speeding the processing of stimuli.

**2.118** Over-inclusive thinking results from weakening of conceptual boundaries.

**2.119** Verbigeration leads to senseless repetition of units of speech.

**2.120** In subjective terms, visual hallucinations are characteristically identical to normal visual stimuli.

**2.121** Discourse analysis can be used to examine speech patterns.

**2.122** Functional hallucinations can only be experienced in the presence of running water.

**2.123** Cross-over studies involve repeated testing of the same individuals.

**2.124** Logistic regression models use continuous response variables.

**2.125** A diagram would be a good example of the use of a descriptive statistical method.

**2.126** Sensitivity is also known as the true negative rate.

**2.127** The null hypothesis is most often used in clinical trials because most are unsuccessful and fail to demonstrate any difference between the groups.

**2.128** WASI is an acronym for Wechsler Assessment of Stable Intelligence.

**2.129** Variance is the square root of the standard deviation.

**2.130** Televised violence may cause aggression in boys because they imitate observed aggression.

**2.131** Ratio scales include a zero point by definition.

**2.132** Cultural factors have an important influence on intelligence.

**2.133** A potential leader's intelligence is more important than their physical attractiveness.

**2.134** Social aspects are important in the formation and maintenance of the concept of the self.

PAPER 2
QUESTIONS

**2.135** Both classical and operant conditioning are important in attitude formation.

**2.136** Antipsychotics occupy D2 receptors within the striatum and the level of receptor occupancy correlates well with their clinical efficacy.

**2.137** Two of the three components of attitudes must be changed before the third component changes in response.

**2.138** Eysenck used orthogonal factor analysis.

**2.139** Sexual behaviour is explained satisfactorily by intrinsic theories of motivation.

**2.140** The James–Lange theory of emotion views emotion in abstract, intellectualised terms.

**2.141** Cytoarchitectural abnormalities have been described in the entorhinal cortex in schizophrenia including disruption of cortical layers.

**2.142** Wilson's disease features autosomal dominant inheritance.

**2.143** The International Classification of Diseases 10th edition (ICD-10) was developed by the World Health Organisation.

**2.144** Pseudohallucination is a term first described by Kunst.

**2.145** Jouvet's model of sleep suggests a monoaminergic-determined pattern.

**2.146** Lesions in the dorsomedial nucleus of the thalamus are seen in Korsakoff's psychosis and are responsible for the memory disorder.

**2.147** The somaesthetic area is located parietally.

**2.148** The arcuate fasciculus links Broca's area and Wernicke's area.

**2.149** Dyslexia is less common in countries using phonetic alphabets.

**2.150** Maslow described both deficiency motivation and growth motivation.

**2.151** Retrobulbar neuritis is also known as optic neuritis.

**2.152** McClelland described the need for achievement.

**2.153** Chronic use of phenytoin causes a folate deficient (microcytic) anaemia.

**2.154** Avoidance learning results from classical rather than operant conditioning.

**2.155** The EEG is abnormal in subdural haematoma and cerebral abscess.

**2.156** Parkes described six stages of bereavement.

**2.157** Biorhythms include circadian, infradian and ultradian rhythm.

**2.158** Neurofibrillary tangles are seen in dementia pugilistica.

**2.159** Dopamine is found in abundance in the cerebellum.

**2.160** Head banging is associated with mental retardation.

**2.161** Harlow worked with infant chimpanzees and demonstrated that feeding has primacy over holding.

**2.162** The theory of reasoned action involves a difference between behavioural intentions and actual behaviour.

**2.163** Diaphoresis is excessive sweating.

**2.164** The motor nucleus of the facial nerve is located in the pons.

**2.165** Schizophrenic thought disorder includes asyndesis.

# EXTENDED MATCHING ITEMS

## 2.166 THEME: GENETICS

| | |
|---|---|
| A | Autosomal dominant |
| B | Autosomal recessive |
| C | Chromosomal aneuploidy |
| D | Incomplete penetrance |
| E | Multifactorial inheritance |
| F | Oligogenic inheritance |
| G | Polygenic inheritance |
| H | Trisomy |
| I | X-linked dominant |
| J | X-linked recessive |

**Choose the item most associated with each of the following diseases from the list above:**

| | |
|---|---|
| 1 | Neurofibromatosis |
| 2 | Hunter's disease |
| 3 | Wilson's disease. |

## 2.167   THEME: PSYCHOPATHOLOGY

| | |
|---|---|
| A | Autochthonous delusion |
| B | Confabulation |
| C | Delusional perception |
| D | Delusion of reference |
| E | Delusional memory |
| F | Nihilistic delusion |
| G | Occupational delusion |
| H | Partial delusion |
| I | Pseudohallucination |
| J | Secondary delusion |

**Choose the most appropriate term from the list above for each of the following:**

1      Arises of out the blue, in a single step and is of direct relevance to the patient.

2      The absolute belief that events, objects or people in the environment have special reference for the patient.

3      A belief that other people are plotting, based on an underlying and pre-existing *wahnstimmung*.

## 2.168 THEME: DEFENCE MECHANISMS

| | |
|---|---|
| A | Acting out |
| B | Displacement |
| C | Idealisation |
| D | Incorporation |
| E | Isolation |
| F | Rationalisation |
| G | Reaction formation |
| H | Regression |
| I | Splitting |
| J | Sublimation |

**Choose the most appropriate term from the list above for each of the following:**

1    The adoption of an attitude in direct opposition to a repressed wish.
2    A form of displacement in which one's real, unacceptable and repressed desire is transformed into a more socially acceptable desire.
3    A dissociative phenomenon allowing recent and traumatic events to be discussed calmly with little affective disturbance.

## 2.169 THEME: BRAIN HORMONES

| | |
|---|---|
| A | Adrenocorticotrophic hormone |
| B | Corticotrophin-releasing factor/corticotrophin-releasing hormone |
| C | DGH |
| D | Follicle-stimulating hormone |
| E | Growth hormone |
| F | Luteinising hormone |
| G | MIH |
| H | Somatostatin |
| I | Thyroid-stimulating hormones |

**Choose the most appropriate hormone from the list above for each of the following:**

1    Released from the anterior pituitary in response to GnRF/GnRH from the hypothalamus.

2    Released from the hypothalamus causing ACTH release from the anterior pituitary.

3    An inhibitory factor released from the hypothalamus causing a fall in plasma levels of GH.

## 2.170 THEME: MOTIVATIONAL THEORIES

A       Cognitive dissonance
B       Cognitive needs
C       Deficiency motivation
D       Esteem needs
E       Extrinsic theories
F       Homeostasis
G       Intrinsic theories
H       Primary biological drives
I       Secondary drives
J       Security needs

**Choose the term from the list above which is best described by each of the following:**

1      Activated by homeostatic imbalance and mediated by brain receptors.

2      Suggest that activities have their own intrinsic rewards and deal with behaviours such as curiosity and play.

3      The highest of the basic needs in Maslow's hierarchy.

## 2.171 THEME: CHROMOSOMAL ABNORMALITIES

| A | Trisomy 3 |
|---|-----------|
| B | Trisomy 4 |
| C | Trisomy 13 |
| D | Trisomy 15 |
| E | Trisomy 17 |
| F | Trisomy 18 |
| G | Trisomy 20 |
| H | Trisomy 19 |
| I | Trisomy 21 |
| J | Trisomy 22 |

**Choose the chromosomal abnormality from the list above which is found in each of the following conditions:**

1     Patau's syndrome
2     Edward's syndrome
3     Down's syndrome

## 2.172   THEME: NEUROPATHOLOGY

A   Alzheimer's disease
B   Binswanger's disease
C   Creutzfeldt–Jakob disease
D   Dementia with Lewy bodies
E   Huntington's disease
F   Parkinson's disease
G   Schizophrenia
H   Vascular dementia
I   Weil's disease
J   Wilson's disease

**Choose the disorder from the list above which is most closely associated with the following neuropathological changes:**

1   A histological triad of spongiform degeneration of grey matter, astrocytic proliferation, neuronal degeneration.
2   Markedly enlarged ventricles due to extensive white matter infarction, especially in periventricular and central areas.
3   Cellular degeneration of the substantia nigra.
4   Neuronal loss, particularly in the caudate and putamen, with normal brain size and Opalski cells.
5   Hirano bodies, granulovacuolar degeneration and generalised cortical atrophy.

## 2.173   THEME: PARIETAL LOBE LESIONS

| | |
|---|---|
| A | Approximate answers |
| B | Contralateral spastic paresis |
| C | Difficulty in drawing complex shapes |
| D | Excessive eating and sexual behaviour, excessive touching of objects, excessive mouthing and inability to interpret visual stimuli |
| E | Impaired learning of new words |
| F | Inability to identify objects by their three-dimensional form |
| G | Loss of ability to determine which finger has been touched |
| H | Red–green colour blindness |
| I | Reduced appreciation of music |
| J | Specific inability to recognise faces |

**Identify the disorder most associated with a lesion in each of the following:**

| | |
|---|---|
| 1 | Contralateral parietal lobe |
| 2 | Dominant parietal lobe |
| 3 | Bilateral parietal lobe. |

# PRACTICE PAPER 2

# Answers

## INDIVIDUAL STATEMENT QUESTIONS

**2.1**  **False** – There is evidence that low levels of alcohol consumption can harm the fetus, with a link to behavioural problems.

**2.2**  **False** – The phenotypes of both parent and child are important. A–Z p240

**2.3**  **True**

**2.4**  **True**

**2.5**  **False** – In adults it leads to acromegaly.

**2.6**  **False** – The prevalence of the condition is also important.

**2.7**  **True** – The consort statement sets standards for randomised controlled trials in an attempt to improve standards. It specifies that the number needed to treat and/or number needed to harm should be made clear.

**2.8**  **False**

**2.9**  **True** A–Z p157

**2.10**  **False** – Placebo medication should not be given to anyone.

**2.11**  **False** – It affects these, as well as serotonin, dopamine and others. A–Z p129–30

**2.12**  **False** – Point prevalence is the proportion of the population who have a disease at a point in time. Incidence is the number of new cases in a specified population over a specified period.

**2.13** **False**
Fear p212

**2.14** **True**

**2.15** **False**

**2.16** **False** – Old asylums, monasteries, large ships and prisons.

**2.17** **False** – South Asian populations have higher rates.

**2.18** **True** – The nature of the relationship is unimportant.

**2.19** **False** – They are prone to confounding because of a lack of controls.

**2.20** **False** – It is only seen in meiosis, which leads to gametogenesis.

**2.21** **True**

**2.22** **True** – This consists of agraphia, dyscalculia, finger agnosia and right–left disorientation.

**2.23** **True**

**2.24** **False** – The EEG is flattened.
A–Z p365–6

**2.25** **False** – Guanine complements cytosine and adenine complements thymine.

**2.26** **False** – Autosomal recessive.

**2.27** **False** – This is a major problem with family studies, where children often have shared environmental experiences.

**2.28** **True** – Including the e2 allele of ApoE, which protects against Alzheimer's disease.

**2.29** **False** – The LOD score is a measure of the likelihood that two genes are linked. They measure linkage between genes or mutations.

**2.30** **True**
A–Z p121–2

**2.31** **False** – Haloperidol is a butyrophenone. The description given applies to piperazines.

**2.32** **False** – Low relative molecular mass increases the speed of absorption.

**2.33** **False** – The posterior fossa is very difficult to image with computed tomography as it is surrounded by bone. Magnetic resonance imaging is the investigation of choice.

**2.34** **False** – The mamillary bodies are an important component of the limbic system.
A–Z p195, Fear p119–20

**2.35** **True**

**2.36** **True**

**2.37** **True** – They cause fragments of differing sizes to be produced when DNA is broken down by restriction enzymes.

**2.38** **True**

**2.39** **False** – The mother is usually the carrier. The father could not be a carrier as he (probably) only has one X chromosome and would therefore express the phenotype.

**2.40** **True** – He described imprinting.

**2.41** **True**

**2.42** **True** – Which is why antipsychotics, with an antidopaminergic action, cause hyperprolactinaemia.

**2.43**    **True**

**2.44**    **True**

**2.45**    **True** – Visual short-term memory is localised to the opposite side.

**2.46**    **True**

**2.47**    **False** – It is about 0.8.

**2.48**    **False** – About 30,000.

**2.49**    **False** – Olanzapine is a thienobenzodiazepine. Aripiprazole is a quinolinone.

**2.50**    **True**

**2.51**    **False** – κ-receptors mediate dysphoria. μ-receptors mediate analgesia, feelings of pleasure and respiratory depression.
Fear p156

**2.52**    **True**
Fear p116

**2.53**    **False** – Serotonin is an indolamine. Catecholamines are monoamines.
A–Z p71, Fear p154–5

**2.54**    **False** – Fragile X syndrome involves CGG repeats.

**2.55**    **True**

**2.56**    **True**

**2.57**    **True** – γ-Aminobutyric acid (GABA) transaminase degrades GABA, which is an inhibitory neurotransmitter. Inhibition of GABA transaminase increases GABA, having a sedative anticonvulsant effect.
A–Z p151, Fear p153

**2.58**  **False** – Few psychotropic drugs have a clear relationship between blood/plasma level and efficacy or toxicity. Examples include clozapine and lithium.

**2.59**  **False** – They are found in the hippocampus and amygdala, in low concentrations.
Fear p155

**2.60**  **True**

**2.61**  **False**

**2.62**  **False**

**2.63**  **True** – α, β and γ

**2.64**  **False** – This is an anti-α₁-adrenergic effect. The main antihistaminergic effect is drowsiness.

**2.65**  **False** – It is competitive.
A–Z p120–2

**2.66**  **False** – It is a G-protein receptor. γ-Aminobutyric acid A (GABA-A) is an ion channel.
Fear p153

**2.67**  **True** – Most commonly in the hippocampus and entorhinal cortex. In the normal brain they are rare, but present in limited areas in small numbers.

**2.68**  **True** – This is mediated by a change in the immune system.

**2.69**  **False** – Well-adjusted and happy elderly people enjoy reminiscing more than the maladjusted elderly.

**2.70**  **True** – Astrocytes are the supportive cells that maintain neurones and the environment around them.

**2.71**  **True** – Although not present at birth, it develops during childhood.

**2.72** **False** – It can be either.

**2.73** **False** – They are seen in the living neurones.

**2.74** **False** – D2, D3 and D4 are similar. D1 and D5 are similar.
Fear p155

**2.75** **False** – There is no fixed half-life with zero-order kinetics.
Fear p145

**2.76** **False** – It was Cade.

**2.77** **True**

**2.78** **False** – Slow-wave sleep increases after exertion or after a longer day than usual.

**2.79** **True** – Damage to the posterior column causes ipsilateral loss of vibration sense, proprioception and tactile discrimination. A–Z p259

**2.80** **True**

**2.81** **False** – There are no liver abnormalities in the child.
A–Z p146 Fear p545–6

**2.82** **True** – Lesions here cause Gerstmann's syndrome, consisting of acalculia, agraphia, finger agnosia and right–left disorientation. Another cause for this syndrome is lesions in the dominant parietal lobe.

**2.83** **False** – The second trimester is most commonly linked to later neurodevelopmental disorders.

**2.84** **True** – Dissocial personality disorder is implicated.

**2.85** **False** – Slow-to-warm-up is a pattern of behaviour relating to temperament, which is largely biologically, rather than psychologically, determined.
A–Z p316

**2.86** **False** – Spikes have a duration of less than 80 ms, waves have a duration greater than 80 ms.

**2.87** **True** – Enzyme deficiencies affecting sex hormones can cause a child with a male genotype to present a female phenotype, and vice versa.

**2.88** **True**

**2.89** **True**

**2.90** **False** – There is a third stage – detachment.
A–Z p211

**2.91** **True** – The act is unimportant, it is the context in which the person views the act.
Fear p82

**2.92** **True**

**2.93** **False** – An individual's social class can change over time and the social classes themselves change. Over the past hundred years, social class 3 (skilled workers) has expanded very significantly in the western world.

**2.94** **True** – The anti-psychiatry movement has been influenced by a number of prominent psychiatrists, most notably Thomas Szasz, a professor of psychiatry.

**2.95** **True** – Parenting tasks appropriate for a neonate (close attention to personal hygiene, feeding, etc) differ from those appropriate for an adolescent (monitoring of inappropriate activities, social education, etc).

**2.96** **True** – Although the social contacts which are maintained are often more rewarding.

**2.97** **False** – This is not the case.

**2.98** **False** – Short-term memory is preserved. Some decline is seen in long-term memory but performance is most affected.

**2.99**   **True** – Both follow the action potential.

**2.100**   **False** – This is Wernicke's area. Broca's area is also known as the motor speech area or the speech association area.
A–Z p367–8

**2.101**   **False** – It is secreted mostly at night, by the pineal gland.

**2.102**   **True**

**2.103**   **True**

**2.104**   **True**
A–Z p199

**2.105**   **True** – They are most prominent when the subject is relaxed.
A–Z p365

**2.106**   **False** – Declarative memory relates to knowledge of discrete facts. Episodic memory concerns events. Both are subtypes of long-term, explicit memory.
A–Z p206–7, Fear p14

**2.107**   **True**
Sims p183

**2.108**   **True** – It then flows through the aqueduct of Sylvius to the fourth ventricle.
Fear p126

**2.109**   **False** – Lewy bodies are found in both Parkinson's disease and Lewy body dementia. Sites characteristic of Lewy body dementia include the cingulated gyrus, parahippocampal gyrus and temporal cortex.

**2.110**   **False** – Existential logotherapy.

**2.111**   **True**

**2.112**   **False** – There are many aspects to both health and illness, which are difficult concepts to define and identify.

**2.113** **True**

**2.114** **True**
Fear p92

**2.115** **False** – It was described by Wolpe.

**2.116** **False** – Affect illusions and completion illusions are more prominent during inattention. Pareidolic illusions become more pronounced when attention is focused on an object. A–Z p176

**2.117** **True** – Concepts are made of the essential characteristics of perceived objects. They are made of attributes, which are the various aspects of a perceived object. Salient attributes are simply the most important attributes. An example is used of a dog. The salient attributes are having four legs, teeth and fur.

**2.118** **True**

**2.119** **True**

**2.120** **True** – The person experiencing them is usually unable to differentiate the hallucination from the normal stimulus.

**2.121** **True**

**2.122** **False** – A functional hallucination is experienced only in association with an unrelated stimulus in the same modality.

**2.123** **True**

**2.124** **False** – The response variable is always a discrete variable, and often with only two values, 0 and 1.

**2.125** **True**

**2.126** **False** – It is the true positive rate. Specificity is known as the true negative rate.

PAPER 2
ANSWERS

**2.127** **False** – The success, or otherwise, of the trial is irrelevant. Fear p70

**2.128** **False** – Wechsler Abbreviated Scale of Intelligence.

**2.129** **False** – It is the square of the standard deviation.

**2.130** **True** – This has been suggested but not proved.

**2.131** **True** – They must include a zero point so that ratios can be calculated.

**2.132** **True** – Different cultures value the various aspects of intelligence in different ways. It is important that tests of intelligence are free from cultural bias.

**2.133** **False** – The most important characteristics of leaders are size, health and attractiveness. Less important are intelligence, confidence and other social characteristics. A–Z p192, Fear p584

**2.134** **True** – Self-concept is derived from both internal and external cues. A–Z p295–6, Fear p30–2, Sims p209–29

**2.135** **True** – Both processes lead to evaluations of stimuli which can become incorporated into attitudes. Fear p27

**2.136** **True**

**2.137** **False** – A change in one component will lead to changes in the other components. There are cognitive, affective and behavioural/conative components. A–Z p49–50

**2.138** **True** A–Z p249

**2.139** **True** – Extrinsic theories describe basic drives such as hunger and thirst, whereas intrinsic theories explain play, addiction, risk-taking and sexual behaviour.

**2.140**   **False** – It explains emotion in purely physical terms.
A–Z p181, Fear p20

**2.141**   **True**

**2.142**   **False** – Autosomal recessive.

**2.143**   **True**
A–Z p175

**2.144**   **False** – Kandinsky.

**2.145**   **True**
A–Z p301

**2.146**   **True**
A–Z p319

**2.147**   **True**
A–Z p43

**2.148**   **True**

**2.149**   **True**

**2.150**   **True**

**2.151**   **True**

**2.152**   **True**

**2.153**   **False** – Macrocytic.
A–Z p252

**2.154**   **False** – It can result from either.
A–Z p193

**2.155**   **True**

**2.156** **False** – He described five stages.

**2.157** **True**
A–Z p61

**2.158** **True**

**2.159** **False**

**2.160** **True**

**2.161** **False** – Holding has primacy over feeding.

**2.162** **True**

**2.163** **True**

**2.164** **True**

**2.165** **True** – This is a disorder of thought which is manifest as fragmentary speech and can lead to speech incoherence.

## EXTENDED MATCHING QUESTIONS

### 2.166   THEME: GENETICS

1        **A** – Autosomal dominant
2        **J** – X-linked recessive
3        **B** – Autosomal recessive.
Fear p185–8

### 2.167   THEME: PSYCHOPATHOLOGY

1        **A** – Autochthonous delusion
2        **D** – Delusion of reference
3        **J** – Secondary delusion.
A–Z p96–7

### 2.168   THEME: DEFENCE MECHANISMS

1        **G** – Reaction formation
2        **J** – Sublimation
3        **E** – Isolation.
A–Z p92–3

### 2.169   THEME: BRAIN HORMONES

1        **F** – Luteinising hormone
2        **B** – Corticotrophin-releasing factor/hormone
3        **H** – Somatostatin, or growth hormone release inhibitory
         factor.

### 2.170   THEME: MOTIVATIONAL THEORIES

1        **H** – Primary biological drives
2        **G** – Intrinsic theories
3        **D** – Esteem needs.
A–Z p203 and 217–18

cont...

PAPER 2
ANSWERS

## 2.171 THEME: CHROMOSOMAL ABNORMALITIES

1   **C** – Trisomy 13
2   **F** – Trisomy 18
3   **I** – Trisomy 21
Fear p381–4

## 2.172 THEME: NEUROPATHOLOGY

1   **C** – Creutzfeldt–Jakob disease
2   **B** – Binswanger's disease
3   **F** – Parkinson's disease
4   **J** – Wilson's disease
5   **A** – Alzheimer's disease

## 2.173 THEME: PARIETAL LOBE LESIONS

1   **F** – Inability to identify objects by their three-dimensional form (astereognosia)
2   **G** – Loss of ability to determine which finger has been touched (finger agnosia)
3   **D** – Excessive eating and sexual behaviour, excessive touching of objects, excessive mouthing and inability to interpret visual stimuli (Kluver–Bucy syndrome)
A–Z p352–3

# PRACTICE PAPER 3

*Time allowed: 90 minutes*

## INDIVIDUAL STATEMENT QUESTIONS

**3.1** Bowlby considered the seeking of proximity, separation distress and the secure-base effect to be suggestive of attachment.

**3.2** Birth asphyxia is associated with schizophrenia.

**3.3** Ethanol has a direct neurotoxic effect on developing fetal neurones.

**3.4** Low maternal socioeconomic background correlates with high prenatal mortality rate.

**3.5** There is clear evidence of a causal link between prenatal exposure to maternal smoking and later antisocial personality disorder.

**3.6** Categories of temperament include quality of mood, intensity of reaction and mild-manneredness.

**3.7** The double-jeopardy hypothesis predicts a particularly poor outcome for elderly persons belonging to other marginal groups.

**3.8** There is a correlation between single-parent families and behavioural and emotional problems.

**3.9** Passive-dependent personality characteristics are appropriate to old age and predict a good adaptation to old age, although there is no evidence of an associated increase in life expectancy.

**3.10** Childhood victims of sexual abuse are less likely to become perpetrators of sexual abuse in later life.

**3.11** Yalom described altruism, catharsis and group intelligence as therapeutic factors within the group.

**3.12** The elderly have few sexual needs, so these do not need to be given consideration when working with the elderly.

**3.13** In a stable group of baboons, the dominant males are consistently aggressive.

**3.14** Children have a more physical self-concept than adults.

**3.15** Mentally well adolescents experience normal emotional states with greater intensity.

**3.16** Attitude–behaviour correspondence varies between individuals.

**3.17** Conditioning is an example of associative learning.

**3.18** The process of forgetting more commonly involves difficulties with retrieval of memories rather than the initial process of storage.

**3.19** Schizophrenia is commonly associated with abnormal pyramid cells in the cerebellum.

**3.20** Autism is characterised by a relative excess of grey matter.

**3.21** Neurofibrillary tangles are seen in Alzheimer's disease.

**3.22** Haptic hallucinations are felt deep inside the body, most commonly in the abdomen.

**3.23** The likelihood ratio is the chance that a negative test result would be expected in a patient with the disorder under study, compared with the likelihood that the same result would be expected in a patient without the target disorder.

**3.24** ABAB studies examine the effects of starting and stopping medication on several, potentially large, groups.

**3.25** Confidence intervals provide an estimated range of values which are unlikely to include the unknown population parameter under examination.

**3.26** Tau protein is absent from cells containing Lewy bodies.

**3.27** The nucleus of the abducens is located in the central medulla.

**3.28** Individuals maintain a number of social roles simultaneously and these change over time.

**3.29** Schizophrenia may be over-diagnosed in people living in the United Kingdom who are of African-Caribbean origin.

**3.30** Exposure to high expressed emotion not only increases the risk of developing schizophrenia, but also increases the risk of subsequent relapse.

**3.31** Freud's concept of the schizophrenogenic mother is now widely discredited.

**3.32** Binary management, involving the splitting of patients into compliant and non-compliant groups, was a concept described by Goffman.

**3.33** The moral and ethical standards used by adolescents to choose potential partners are usually in direct opposition to those of their parents.

**3.34** Block and Haan identified the 'dominating narcissist' as a type of male adolescent.

**3.35** Thyrotrophin-releasing hormone increases prolactin secretion.

**3.36** People with mental illness should not be allowed to drive.

**3.37** Some clozapine is excreted unchanged in the urine.

**3.38** Confidence intervals are associated with odds ratios.

**3.39** Individual needs assessment is complicated and specific to individuals. It can only be done on a case-by-case basis and should avoid the use of standardised assessment tools.

**3.40** Detained patients do not have to give informed consent as long as their doctor is acting in their best interests.

**3.41** Imprinting results from intrauterine environmental effects causing irreversible changes to the developing DNA.

**3.42** Teleological ethics judge actions in themselves, rather than what the actions achieve.

**3.43** Semi-structured questionnaires are much easier and quicker to score than structured questionnaires.

**3.44** A survey is an example of a cross-sectional study.

**3.45** The 3' non-coding region contains a poly A addition site.

**3.46** Cross-sectional studies enable an accurate measurement of the incidence of common psychiatric disorders.

**3.47** Linkage describes the fact that two genes located near to each other are always inherited together.

**3.48** Neurofibromatosis is a sex-linked disorder.

**3.49** Fragile X syndrome results from an abnormality at Xq 26.

**3.50** Tests with a predetermined pass mark are often norm-referenced.

**3.51** The relationship of the tester and the subject can affect the results of intelligence tests.

**3.52** Dependent variables are those which depend on manipulation by the person designing the study.

**3.53** Altruism is defined as giving or sharing with others when there is obvious gain and may take the form of words or actions.

**3.54** Reciprocal inhibition involves systematic desensitisation to a hierarchy of increasingly anxiogenic stimuli, which can be real or imaginary.

**3.55** Cri-du-chat syndrome results from the partial deletion of 5q.

**3.56** Second-degree relatives share 50% of their genes.

**3.57** Penetrance is the extent to which a particular recessive gene is expressed.

**3.58** Allergic drug reactions are dose-related.

**3.59** There is an association between G-proteins and phosphatidylinositol-specific phospholipase.

**3.60** Effective drugs are characteristically distributed between the three compartments of the body in equal measure.

**3.61** Acetylcholine receptors can be nicotinic or muscarinic and come in many different forms.

**3.62** Autosomal dominant disorders which fail to manifest in a generation but reappear in a later generation may do so as a result of incomplete penetrance.

**3.63** Lesch–Nyhan syndrome is an X-linked dominant disorder.

**3.64** Aggressive and impulsive behaviour can result from discontinuation of a selective serotonin reuptake inhibitor (SSRI).

**3.65** Patients taking monoamine oxidase inhibitors should avoid alcohol.

**3.66** Polygenic disorders are inherited in Mendelian fashion.

**3.67** The vast majority of the human genome consists of non-coding 'junk' DNA.

**3.68** Adverse drug reactions are generally idiosyncratic and difficult to predict.

**3.69** Clozapine has effects on serotonin 2 receptors.

**3.70** Janov wrote *The Primal Scream*.

**3.71** Adrenocorticotrophic hormone is produced from pro-opiomelanocortin and causes production of glucocorticoids such as cortisol, and mineralocorticoids such as aldosterone and androgens.

**3.72** The supraoptic area within the anterior pituitary secretes antidiuretic hormone and oxytocin.

**3.73** Cognitive estimation may be reduced following a frontal lobe lesion.

**3.74** Intravenous administration is advantageous because it reduces first-pass metabolism.

**3.75** EEG changes in Angelman's syndrome include large-amplitude slow-spike waves.

**3.76** Theta rhythms are fast waves at 4–8 Hz.

**3.77** Prolactin is secreted mainly at night, whereas growth hormone is secreted mainly during the day.

**3.78** Dopamine is a precursor of noradrenaline.

**3.79** The locus caeruleus primarily contains serotonergic neurones.

**3.80** The therapeutic effects of atypical antipsychotics correlate with the extent of their dopamine D4 blockade.

**3.81** Phenytoin is a hepatic enzyme inducer that reduces the concentration of tricyclic antidepressants.

**3.82** Drug discontinuation reactions indicate that commonly used antidepressants are addictive.

**3.83** Reversible inhibitors of monoamine oxidase allow the patient to eat unlimited quantities of cheese without concern.

**3.84** Becker suggested that a person is deviant not as a result of his actions, but as a result of the way they are interpreted.

**3.85** Core family concepts vary according to time and place.

**3.86** Marx believed that different social classes generally complemented each other and lived in harmony.

**3.87** Despair is one of the six primary emotions described by Plutchik.

**3.88** Serotonin IA receptors are found in pre- and postsynaptic locations.

**3.89** Transport across the placenta can only occur by active transport.

**3.90** The volume of distribution of a drug correlates positively with its duration of action.

**3.91** Corticotrophin-releasing hormone increases plasma glucose concentrations whilst inhibiting feeding and sexual behaviour.

**3.92** Ionotropic receptors commonly have five subunits, as seen in the $\gamma$-aminobutyric acid receptor.

**3.93** Alcohol has a low therapeutic index.

**3.94** A lesion in the lateral hypothalamus may result in excessive thirst.

**3.95** Synaptic transmission in humans is unusual as it is often bi-directional.

**3.96** As a result of the intense magnetic fields generated by single photon emission computed tomography (SPECT) scanners, people with ferromagnetic implants cannot be scanned.

**3.97** Carbamazepine was used as an anticonvulsant before its introduction as a mood stabiliser.

**3.98** The actions of antipsychotic drugs have led to the development of the dopamine hypothesis of schizophrenia.

**3.99** Haloperidol was synthesised by Delay and Deniker in 1932.

**3.100** Monoamine oxidase inhibitors were introduced in 1967.

**3.101** Magnetic resonance imaging has a resolution of 0.1 mm.

**3.102** Mesial temporal sclerosis has a causal link with atypical seizures.

**3.103** The reward effects of stimulants are mediated by the mesolimbic–mesocortical pathway.

**3.104** Thioxanthene antipsychotics are closely related to phenothiazines.

**3.105** Phenelzine is a hydrazine monoamine oxidase inhibitor.

**3.106** Elevated prolactin levels are associated with failure of both erection and ejaculation.

**3.107** Autoreceptors are presynaptic and are located on the same neurone that produces the neurotransmitter.

**3.108** Cortical sensory loss involves items being perceived but not recognised.

**3.109** Phencyclidine acts on NMDA receptors to cause symptoms similar to those of schizophrenia.

**3.110** End-stage renal failure causes a clinically significant reduction in growth hormone levels.

**3.111** The mamillary bodies have an important role in memory.

**3.112** Lambda rhythms are seen in occipital regions when the eyes are open.

**3.113** In a neurone at rest, the potassium level will be relatively low.

**3.114** Alpha rhythms, with frequencies of 8–13 Hz, usually originate from the front of the brain.

**3.115** Child sexual abuse can lead to paranoia.

**3.116** Crystallised intelligence increases with age, so older adults can present with greater verbal fluency.

**3.117** Cerebral hemispheric symmetry is reduced in schizophrenia.

**3.118** The repeated measures design avoids difficulties in interpretation by measuring a single group of subjects repeatedly under different conditions.

**3.119** Bilateral temporal lobe lesions cause confabulation, whereas unilateral lesions only ever cause difficulty in planning tasks.

**3.120** Damage to neurones by free radicals is implicated in the pathogenesis of tardive dyskinesia.

**3.121** Perseveration is pathognomonic of organic brain disease.

**3.122** The social drift hypothesis explains why schizophrenia is more prevalent in Eastern Europe than in South America.

**3.123** Parkinson's disease leads to severe depletion of dopamine in the substantia nigra, with up to 95% dopamine loss.

**3.124** Neuropathological changes in Parkinson's disease affect the reticular formation.

**3.125** The presentation of a given disorder varies according to culture.

**3.126** Patients who report poor social support are more likely to experience depressive symptoms.

**3.127** The incidence of death shortly after retirement is higher in lower social classes.

**3.128** Perinatal death is more grief-inducing than sudden infant death.

**3.129** Doctors are obliged by their social role to impose a diagnosis of illness, even when the patient is reluctant to accept this.

**3.130** Hallucinations are self-referent.

**3.131** Aphonia is the loss of ability to use the telephone.

**3.132** The type–token ratio rises significantly in schizophrenia.

**3.133** The mean is a good measure of central tendency, especially with small datasets and multiple outliers.

**3.134** Women have a predisposition to tardive dyskinesia.

**3.135** Sorting tests can test for over-inclusive thinking.

**3.136** Bateson described double-blind studies.

**3.137** Perceptual set is determined by motivation and emotion, but is independent of cultural factors.

**3.138** Unlike salient attributes, cores are not always required for a concept to be interpreted correctly.

**3.139** The Q sort technique allows comparisons of traits between individuals.

**3.140** Cognitive dissonance, described by Falret, explains motivation in terms of discomfort experienced when two or more inconsistent cognitions are held, which are in conflict with one another.

**3.141** Groups show more restraint than individuals.

**3.142** Lesions in the angular gyrus are associated with inability to read and write.

**3.143** Griesinger described unitary psychosis and primary insanity.

**3.144** Babbling is independent of learning or culture.

**3.145** Kline reported on the use of selective serotonin reuptake inhibitors (SSRIs) in depression.

**3.146** Gustatory and olfactory hallucinations can occur together in schizophrenia.

**3.147** Obsessive-compulsive disorder is characterised by dysregulation of serotonin and dopamine.

**3.148** Korsakoff's psychosis is better understood as a chronic memory disorder than as a true psychosis.

**3.149** Hypochondriacal disorder is classified with somatoform disorders in the 10th edition of the International Classification of Diseases (ICD-10).

**3.150** Enteric coating of oral medication causes absorption to occur from the small rather than the large bowel.

**3.151** Positron emission tomography (PET) allows the study of regional cerebral blood flow more effectively than magnetic resonance imaging, even when a T2 scan is performed.

**3.152** Voluntary movement is brought about by the frontal lobe in the first instance.

**3.153** Freud described defence mechanisms as unconscious and pathological.

**3.154** Oligodendrocytes form myelin sheaths.

**3.155** Oligogenic inheritance is Mendelian.

**3.156** The medulla oblongata contains the nucleus of cranial nerve XII.

**3.157** Mayer-Gross described need for achievement.

**3.158** Melatonin is released from the pineal gland and acts at the raphe nucleus to increase serotonin production.

**3.159** Active placebos contain substances which mimic the side-effects of the active drug.

**3.160** Punning is a type of loosening of association characteristically seen in schizophrenia.

**3.161** Freud describes the id as entirely unconscious.

**3.162** Pairing is guided by homogamous mate selection.

**3.163** Learning can occur by association and by classical or operant conditioning.

**3.164** Interactionism aims to present a complete account of the human condition.

**3.165** Rifampicin is a hepatic enzyme inducer.

# EXTENDED MATCHING ITEMS

### 3.166  THEME: ERIKSON'S THEORY OF DEVELOPMENT

| | |
|---|---|
| A | Angst versus acceptance |
| B | Autonomy versus shame and doubt |
| C | Generativity versus stagnation |
| D | Identity versus confusion |
| E | Industry versus inferiority |
| F | Initiative versus guilt |
| G | Integrity versus despair |
| H | Intimacy versus isolation |
| I | Superiority versus sensitivity |
| J | Trust versus mistrust |

**Choose the most appropriate of Erikson's developmental stages from the list above for each of the following descriptions:**

1    Success in this first stage leads to trust in the environment and hope for the future.

2    This stage involves initial exploration of the environment and one's sexuality and failure leads to fear of punishment and guilt as a result of one's own feelings.

3    There is continued growth and development. If successful, productivity is maintained and a contribution to society is made.

PAPER 3
QUESTIONS

## 3.167 THEME: DRUG CLASSIFICATION

| | |
|---|---|
| A | Clozapine |
| B | Duloxetine |
| C | Olanzapine |
| D | Pimozide |
| E | Risperidone |
| F | Sulpiride |
| G | Thioridazine |
| H | Tranycypromine |
| I | Venlafaxine |
| J | Zopiclone |

Choose the drug from the above list which fits into each of these categories:

| | |
|---|---|
| 1 | Cyclopyrrolones |
| 2 | Benzisoxamoles |
| 3 | Diphenylbutylpiperidines. |

## 3.168   THEME: DEVELOPMENT OF LANGUAGE

| | |
|---|---|
| A | Adulthood |
| B | 0–12 hours |
| C | 3 months |
| D | 4 months |
| E | 9 months |
| F | 12 months |
| G | 18 months |
| H | 2 years |
| I | 3 years |
| J | 8 years |

**Choose the most appropriate timescale from the list above for the development of each of the following:**

1    Ability to distinguish mother's voice
2    Repetitive babbling
3    Holophrastic speech.

## 3.169  THEME: NEUROPSYCHOLOGICAL TESTS

| | |
|---|---|
| A | Digit span |
| B | Folstein MMSE |
| C | ITEM |
| D | Kimler–Steiner Test |
| E | National Adult Reading Test (NART) |
| F | Rorschach |
| G | Wechsler Abbreviated Scale of Intelligence (WASI) |
| H | Wechsler Adult Intelligence Scale 3rd version (WAIS-III) |
| I | Wechsler Intelligence Scale Children third version (WISC-III) |
| J | Wisconsin Card Sorting Test |

**A 24-year-old man is referred to you. He has a history of head injury following a motorcycle accident 6 months previously.**

| | |
|---|---|
| 1 | Which is the quickest and most convenient test of his intelligence? |
| 2 | Which test would measure his premorbid IQ? |
| 3 | Which is the best test of immediate memory? |

## 3.170 THEME: TYPES OF MEMORY

| | |
|---|---|
| A | Declarative memory |
| B | Dissociative memory |
| C | Explicit memory |
| D | Iconic memory |
| E | Priming |
| F | Proactive interference |
| G | Procedural memory |
| H | Retroactive interference |
| I | Short-term memory |
| J | State-dependent learning |

**Choose the most appropriate term from the list above for each of the following:**

1    The type of memory involved in learning to ride a bicycle.
2    Learning new information is difficult because something similar, but slightly different, has already been learnt.
3    The capacity to profit from prior exposure to clues such as partially completed words when performing an executive task.

### 3.171 THEME: ASCENDING SPINAL TRACTS AND SYNDROMES

A      Anterior spinocerebellar tract
B      Anterior spinothalamic tract
C      Fasciculus cuneatus
D      Fasciculus gracilis
E      Fasciculus medialis
F      Lateral spinocerebellar tract
G      Lateral spinothalamic tract
H      Posterior spinocerebellar tract
I      Spino-olivary tract
J      Spinotectal tract

**Choose the spinal tract from the list above which conveys signals relating to the following stimuli:**

1      Light touch and pressure
2      Discriminative touch and proprioception
3      Vibration.

## 3.172 THEME: PIAGET'S DEVELOPMENTAL THEORY

| | |
|---|---|
| A | Animism |
| B | Artificialism |
| C | Authoritarian morality |
| D | Creationism |
| E | Deontological approach |
| F | Egocentricity |
| G | Precausal reasoning |
| H | Realism |
| I | Teleological approach |
| J | Transductive reasoning |

**Identify the term from the list above which best describes the thinking process underlying each of the following statements:**

1    If I dream it or imagine it, it must exist. There is no boundary between fantasy and reality.

2    The toys on the bed have feelings just like everybody else.

3    Insects and birds can both fly, so they must be identical.

4    Nothing happens by chance in this world. If it rains and I get cold and wet, I must have done something wrong.

## 3.173 THEME: HERITABILITY

A     Angelman's syndrome
B     Edward's syndrome
C     Familial Alzheimer's disease
D     Galactosaemia
E     Hunter's disease
F     Lesch–Nyhan syndrome
G     Patau's syndrome
H     Prader–Willi syndrome
I     Tay–Sachs disease
J     Tuberous sclerosis

**Choose the two conditions from the above list with the following patterns of heritability:**

1     Autosomal dominant
2     Autosomal recessive
3     X-linked recessive.

# PRACTICE PAPER 3

# Answers

## INDIVIDUAL STATEMENT QUESTIONS

**3.1**     **True** – These were the core behaviours of attachment and were also thought to have survival value.

**3.2**     **True** – There is a strong association.

**3.3**     **True**

**3.4**     **True**

**3.5**     **False** – There may be an association but no causal link has been demonstrated. Findings regarding the effects of smoking are confounded by other variables.

**3.6**     **False** – There are nine in total and mild-manneredness does not feature.
See A–Z p316 for a full list.

**3.7**     **True** – The alternative view is the 'age as leveller' hypothesis which suggests that all the elderly are disadvantaged, so the effects of further disadvantage as a result of ethnicity, gender or other characteristics are less noticeable.

**3.8**     **True**

**3.9**     **False** – Passive-dependent personalities predict poor outcome in the elderly.

**3.10**     **False** – There is a positive correlation between childhood experience of sexual abuse and later perpetration of abuse.

**3.11**     **False** – Altruism, catharsis and group cohesiveness. The other factors making up the 11 factors are: installation of hope, universality, imparting of information, interpersonal learning, the corrective recapitulation of the primary family group, development of socialising techniques, imitative behaviour and existential factors.

**3.12** **False** – It is important to treat all patients holistically, including the elderly. Their needs in terms of relationships are often neglected, having a negative impact on their mental health.

**3.13** **True** – They maintain their high status by aggression to less dominant members of the group, including females.

**3.14** **True** – Adults define self-concept largely in terms of their role. Self-concept was classically defined by Rogers as 'a set of attitudes one holds about oneself, not necessarily corresponding with reality'.
A–Z p295, Fear p30, Sims p209–10

**3.15** **True** – This is part of Hall's theory of adolescence, which proposes that each individual's development is a re-enactment of the process of human evolution.

**3.16** **True** – the extent to which individuals self-monitor and the nature of the perceived locus of control have an influence on attitude–behaviour correspondence.
Fear p28

**3.17** **True**
A–Z p79, Fear p3–6

**3.18** **True**
A–Z p207

**3.19** **False** – The abnormal pyramid cells are seen in the hippocampus.

**3.20** **False** – There is a relative excess of white matter, which grows abnormally quickly during the first few years of life.

**3.21** **True**

**3.22** **False** – They are superficial. Visceral hallucinations are deep.

Both are forms of tactile hallucination.

**3.23** **False** – This would be true if you change the word 'negative' on the first line to 'positive'.

**3.24** **False** – ABAB studies are conducted on one group.

**3.25** **False** – The confidence interval is likely to include the parameter.

**3.26** **False** – Tau protein is found in Lewy bodies.

**3.27** **False** – It is found in the pons.
A–Z p258

**3.28** **True**

**3.29** **True**

**3.30** **True** – Risk of relapse in a given period can be increased up to four-fold if a patient is subject to high expressed emotion.

**3.31** **False** – The idea is discredited, but was described by Fromm-Reichmann.

**3.32** **False** – Binary management was described by Goffman, but involves patients and staff being in different groups.

**3.33** **False** – Contrary to popular belief, adolescents share most of their views and judgements about the world with their parents. This was examined by a classical study by Offer and Offer. Children with 'warm' parents are more likely to accept their parents' values and share them later in life.
A–Z p6–8

**3.34** **False** – The dominating narcissist was a type of female adolescent, along with the female prototype, the cognitive type, the hyperfeminine repressor, the vulnerable under-controller and the lonely independent.
A–Z p7–8

**3.35** **True**

**3.36** **False**

**3.37** **True** – About 5%.

**3.38** **True**

**3.39** **False** – Standardised tools such as the Camberwell Assessment of Need are useful.

**3.40** **False** – There are procedures which allow medication to be given to detained patients but they are designed to avoid one doctor having control over a patient's medication.

**3.41** **False** – Imprinting describes the situation occurring when genes are expressed differently depending on whether they are inherited from the mother or the father.

**3.42** **False** – Teleology justifies actions in terms of what they achieve. 'The end justifies the means.'

**3.43** **False** – Structured questionnaires are the easiest to score but are limited in other ways.
Fear p215

**3.44** **True**

**3.45** **True**

**3.46** **False**
Fear p211

**3.47** **False** – They are usually inherited together, but not always.

**3.48** **False** – It is autosomal recessive.

**3.49** **False** – The abnormality is at Xp 27.3. Lesch–Nyhan syndrome has an abnormality at Xq 26.

**3.50** **False** – They are criterion-referenced.

**3.51**  **True**

**3.52**  **False** – This describes independent variables. The dependent variables are those which constitute the results of the study.

**3.53**  **False** – Altruism involves no obvious gain.

**3.54**  **True** – Systematic desensitisation is the process of relaxing whilst being exposed to phobic stimuli, which reduces the anxigenic effects of the phobic stimuli.

**3.55**  **False** – It is caused by deletion of 5p.

**3.56**  **False** – They share 25%.

**3.57**  **False** – This is true only for dominant genes.

**3.58**  **False** – Even small doses can cause severe anaphylactic reactions.

**3.59**  **True**

**3.60**  **False** – The three compartments are lipids, proteins and water, and drugs are distributed unequally between them.

**3.61**  **True**

**3.62**  **True**

**3.63**  **False** – It is X-linked recessive.

**3.64**  **True**

**3.65**  **False** – Alcohol (ethanol) presents no special risks, but beer and some particular types of wine should be avoided. A–Z p213–14

**3.66**  **False** – They are not inherited in the classical Mendelian fashion. An example of a polygenic disorder is schizophrenia.

**3.67**  **True** – Over 95%.

**3.68** **False** – They are classified as intolerance, idiosyncratic, allergic or relating to drug interactions.

**3.69** **True** – Serotonin 2, dopamine 1 and 4, acetylcholinergic, muscarinic and α-adrenergic receptors.

**3.70** **True** – He also developed primal therapy.

**3.71** **True**

**3.72** **False** – This area is within the hypothalamus.

**3.73** **True**

**3.74** **True**
A–Z p179–80

**3.75** **True**

**3.76** **False** – They have a frequency of 4–8 Hz, which makes them slow waves.

**3.77** **False** – They are both secreted mostly at night.

**3.78** **True**

**3.79** **False** – Noradrenergic neurones.

**3.80** **False** – Their dopamine D2 blockade.

**3.81** **True** – Other drugs having the same effect include barbiturates and rifampicin.

**3.82** **False** – Discontinuation reactions and dependence are different, according to the International Classification of Diseases 10th edition (ICD-10) criteria.

**3.83** **False** – Large quantities of tyramine-containing foods are liable to cause mild versions of 'the cheese effect' but most often a normal diet can be taken.

**3.84**    **True** – This is a consequence of social labelling theory.
Fear p82

**3.85**    **True** – The nature of the family has changed over recent years, and varies in different parts of the world.

**3.86**    **False** – The idea of the class struggle was central to Marxist ideology.

**3.87**    **False** – Plutchik's eight primary emotions are acceptance, anger, anticipation/expectancy, disgust, fear, joy/happiness, sadness and surprise.
A–Z p132–3

**3.88**    **True**
Fear p156

**3.89**    **False** – Transport across the placenta also occurs by passive diffusion and pinocytosis.
A–Z p120–2

**3.90**    **False** – There is an inverse relationship.
A–Z p120–2

**3.91**    **True** – It also increases blood pressure and pulse.

**3.92**    **True**
Fear p152

**3.93**    **True** – The ratio of the therapeutic dose to the toxic dose is so low that if it were a drug, it would not be licensed, because of the danger of overdosage.

**3.94**    **True** – Thirst is controlled here and a lesion may result in either deficiency or excess.

**3.95**    **False** – It is always unidirectional.

**3.96**    **False** – This applies to magnetic resonance imaging.

**3.97**    **True**

**3.98** **True**

**3.99** **False** – It was synthesised by Janssen in 1958.

**3.100** **False** – 1958.

**3.101** **False** – 1 mm.

**3.102** **True** – Temporal lobe epilepsy.

**3.103** **True**

**3.104** **True** – Both in structure and in terms of their clinical profile. They are associated with increased appetite and weight gain.

**3.105** **True** – Isocarboxazid is also in this category.

**3.106** **True** – They also cause reduced libido.

**3.107** **True**
Fear p152

**3.108** **True** – This occurs in parietal lobe dysfunction.

**3.109** **True**
A–Z p225

**3.110** **False** – It increases growth hormone levels, but not in a clinically significant manner.

**3.111** **True**

**3.112** **True** – They are related to eye movements during visual inattention.

**3.113** **False** – Resting neurones are characterised by high potassium levels, with low sodium and chloride. There is a strong negative charge inside the cell.

**3.114** **False** – They arise posteriorly.

**3.115** **True** –There are many consequences of child sexual abuse, including anxiety, post-traumatic stress disorder, depressive disorders, dissociative disorders, personality disorders and many others.
A–Z p2–3

**3.116** **True** – Crystallised intelligence increases with age, leading to better experience-based judgement as well as more able and complex patterns of speech.

**3.117** **True**

**3.118** **True**

**3.119** **False** – Unilateral lesions also cause impaired learning of new words (dominant side) and reduced appreciation of music (non-dominant side).

**3.120** **True** – This is a theory, but the concept of dopamine hypersensitivity is widely believed to be more important.

**3.121** **True** – This is almost the only case in which a sign is pathognomonic of anything in psychiatry!

**3.122** **False** – The prevalence rate for schizophrenia is approximately equal in every area of the world. The social drift hypothesis proposes that people with mental illness (particularly schizophrenia) move down through the social classes as a result of their illness. It explains why the prevalence rate of schizophrenia is higher in lower social classes.

**3.123** **True**

**3.124** **True**

**3.125** **True** – Cultural variation has an important influence on the presentation of mental illness.

**3.126** **True** – This is explained by the buffering model of social support.

PAPER 3
ANSWERS

**3.127** **True** – It is approximately twice as high in social class 5 as in social class 1.

**3.128** **False** – The reverse is true.

**3.129** **True** – This is described by Mechanic as forming part of illness behaviour, related to the sick role.

**3.130** **True** – They have special meaning for the person experiencing them in the overwhelming majority of cases.

**3.131** **False** – It is the loss of the ability to vocalise.

**3.132** **False** – This is a measure of the complexity of speech patterns, measured as the number of different words as a proportion of the total number of words. The complexity of speech (and therefore the type–token ratio) falls in schizophrenia.

**3.133** **False** – The median is a good measure in this situation. The mean is likely to be unreliable.

**3.134** **True**

**3.135** **True**

**3.136** **False** – He described double-bind communication.

**3.137** **False** – Perceptual set causes stimuli to be perceived and interpreted in accordance with one's expectations. Cultural factors have an influence on this process.

**3.138** **False** – Salient attributes are simply the most important aspects of a perceived object. Cores are aspects of it which must be present for the perceived object to be interpreted correctly as belonging to a group. For example, the salient attributes pertaining to rain clouds are largeness and greyness. Rain clouds can be small and white, however. A core feature of rain clouds is that they occur in the sky. If a potential rain cloud is found anywhere else, then it cannot possibly be a rain cloud. Salient attributes are important, cores are essential.

**3.139** **False** – It is specifically for the comparison of different traits within an individual and is not appropriate for comparing traits between individuals.

**3.140** **False** – This is true, except that cognitive dissonance was described by Festinger. Falret described *folie circulaire*.

**3.141** **False** – They show less restraint.

**3.142** **True**

**3.143** **True**

**3.144** **True**
A–Z p55

**3.145** **False** – He reported on monoamine oxidase inhibitors (MAOIs).

**3.146** **True**

**3.147** **True**
Fear p247

**3.148** **True**

**3.149** **True**

**3.150** **False** – The reverse is true.

**3.151** **True** – Magnetic resonance imaging does not allow the study of regional cerebral blood flow.

**3.152** **True** – In the primary motor cortex of the frontal lobe.
Fear p127

**3.153** **False** – He said they were unconscious and adaptive rather than pathological.

**3.154** **True**
Fear p139

**3.155** **False**
Fear p181

**3.156** **True** – This is the hypoglossal nerve.

**3.157** **False** – That was McClelland. Mayer-Gross described oneirophrenia.

**3.158** **True**

**3.159** **True**

**3.160** **False** – It is seen in mania.

**3.161** **False** – This is a difficult question that can be argued over at length. The consensus is that the id is mostly unconscious and the ego mainly conscious.

**3.162** **True**
A–Z p235

**3.163** **True** – It can also occur by cognitive learning and observational learning.

**3.164** **True** – Although it acknowledges that this will take time.

**3.165** **True** – It is an antibiotic.

# EXTENDED MATCHING ITEMS

### 3.166 THEME: ERIKSON'S THEORY OF DEVELOPMENT

1    **J** – Trust versus mistrust (0–1 years)
2    **F** – Initiative versus guilt (3–6 years)
3    **C** – Generativity versus stagnation (40–64 years)
A–Z p138–9

### 3.167 THEME: DRUG CLASSIFICATION

1    **J** – Zopiclone
2    **E** – Risperidone
3    **D** – Pimozide

### 3.168 THEME: DEVELOPMENT OF LANGUAGE

1    **B** – This occurs within hours of birth.
2    **E** – This occurs at 8–9 months.
3    **F** – This occurs at 12 months. It is the use of single word utterances with varying inflection and gesture to convey a range of meanings.
A–Z p190–1

### 3.169 THEME: NEUROPSYCHOLOGICAL TESTS

1    **G** – The WASI is the Wechsler Abbreviated Scale of Intelligence.
2    **E** – The National Adult Reading Test measures skills relating to language and vocabulary, which give an estimate of verbal IQ. A discrepancy between verbal and performance IQ may relate to head injury or other relatively recent impairment acquired in adult life.
3    **A** – Digit span is a specific test for immediate memory.

### 3.170 THEME: TYPES OF MEMORY

1    **G** – Procedural memory
2    **F** – Proactive interference
3    **E** – Priming

PAPER 3
ANSWERS

### 3.171 THEME: ASCENDING SPINAL TRACTS AND SYNDROMES

1     **B** – Anterior spinothalamic tract
2     **C** – Fasciculus cuneatus
3     **D** – Fasciculus gracilis

### 3.172 THEME: PIAGET'S DEVELOPMENTAL THEORY

1     **H** – Realism
2     **A** – Animism
3     **J** – Transductive reasoning
4     **B** – Artificialism

### 3.173 THEME: HERITABILITY

1     **C & J** – Familial Alzheimer's disease and Tuberous sclerosis
2     **D & I** – Galactosaemia and Tay–Sachs disease
3     **E & F** – Hunter's disease and Lesch–Nyhan syndrome

# PRACTICE PAPER 4

*Time allowed: 90 minutes*

## INDIVIDUAL STATEMENT QUESTIONS

**4.1**   Attachment persists throughout life and is exacerbated by stress and illness.

**4.2**   Autism is associated with enlargement of the amygdala.

**4.3**   Non-dominant temporal lobe lesions cause prosopagnosia and hemisomatognosia.

**4.4**   Neuroendocrine hormonal production in humans is relatively constant.

**4.5**   Duloxetine is a serotonin/noradrenaline reuptake inhibitor, acting as an antidepressant.

**4.6**   Autoreceptors are commonly involved in limited positive feedback loops.

**4.7**   Children of permissive parents have low social and cognitive competencies.

**4.8**   Monsters present a source of fear for an average 4-year-old child.

**4.9**   Elderly people reviewing their lifetime achievements can achieve ego integrity.

**4.10**   Older adults sleep more than younger adults.

**4.11**   Olsen described the circumference model of the family.

**4.12**   Triangulation involves the use of several different approaches to a problem to address it more accurately.

**4.13** P-values are descriptive statistics.

**4.14** Thought echo, described by Carl Schneider and also known as *gedankenlautwerden*, is experienced as one's own thoughts being repeated aloud.

**4.15** Elderly men generally experience less short-wave sleep than elderly women.

**4.16** Noradrenergic α₂ receptors are post-synaptic.

**4.17** Glutamate is an excitatory neurotransmitter of clinical significance.

**4.18** An example of a metabotropic glutamate receptor would be the NMDA receptor.

**4.19** Chronic parental discord and/or separation can have more severe consequences for a child than uniparental death.

**4.20** A parent's sex hormones have a significant effect on their parenting style.

**4.21** The ability of a child to form an attachment is determined to a great extent by the child's experience of parenting.

**4.22** Dopamine D1 and D5 receptors are similar.

**4.23** Vasopressin is a peptide.

**4.24** Peptide neurotransmitters include secretin.

**4.25** Hyperprolactinaemia has several negative effects on sexual arousal.

**4.26** Suppression of the dorsomedial hypothalamic nuclear region produces a feeling of satiety.

**4.27** Wallenberg's syndrome causes contralateral loss of pain and temperature sensitivity.

**4.28**   Somatostatin increases production of thyroid-stimulating hormone in the anterior lobe of the pituitary.

**4.29**   Coarse tremor is a side-effect of lithium at therapeutic doses.

**4.30**   Impending death is experienced through four stages: of denial, anger, depression and acceptance.

**4.31**   Durkheim worked on suicide but his ideas can be extrapolated to other forms of illness.

**4.32**   Transactional analysis understands social interactions in terms of stimuli and responses.

**4.33**   A person refused a job because of a mental illness has been subject to enacted stigma.

**4.34**   Demographic changes in population characteristics must be taken into account when planning the provision of psychiatric services.

**4.35**   Common effects of the discontinuation syndrome seen with selective serotonin reuptake inhibitors (SSRIs) include nausea and headache.

**4.36**   Lithium inhibits cAMP and phosphoinositol second-messenger generating systems.

**4.37**   Giving several antipsychotics at low doses helps to reduce side-effects while preserving the therapeutic effect.

**4.38**   Dopamine agonism in the nigrostriatal pathway causes extrapyramidal symptoms.

**4.39**   *Hypericum perforatum* is an alternative medicine which has few, if any, effects on the brain.

**4.40**   Kappa receptors have a role in dysphoria.

**4.41**   The rate of drug absorption is dependent on the particle size of the drug and the ambient pH.

**4.42** Translation involves the production of tRNA and cRNA.

**4.43** Groupthink is more prominent when there is ample time to achieve the objective.

**4.44** Maternal alcohol consumption during pregnancy correlates with prenatal mortality, even when maternal smoking and socioeconomic background have been adequately controlled for.

**4.45** Down's syndrome can be caused by a translocation.

**4.46** No psychiatric disorders have autosomal dominant inheritance patterns.

**4.47** If an autosomal recessive disorder affects both parents, who are carriers, then one in eight of their children will exhibit the phenotype of the disorder.

**4.48** Learning of motor skills is associated with the basal ganglia.

**4.49** Tay–Sachs disease is inherited as an autosomal recessive disorder and manifests itself as a glycogen storage disease.

**4.50** Huntington's disease is sex-linked.

**4.51** Magnetic resonance imaging has a similar resolution to single photon emission computed tomography.

**4.52** Speed of transmission of an action potential is a function of the diameter of the neurone.

**4.53** Jouvet's model suggests that sleep is controlled partly by serotonergic neurones.

**4.54** Characteristic abnormalities are seen in P300 evoked potentials in schizophrenia.

**4.55** There are usually 48 pairs of chromosomes in humans, represented by 46 XY or 46 XX.

**4.56** Drug reactions resulting from intolerance result from known pharmacological actions of the drug.

**4.57** Anaphylactic reactions are type II hypersensitivity reactions.

**4.58** Semantic functions are performed by the left temporal lobe.

**4.59** Central muscarinic blockade caused by psychotropic drugs causes the side-effects of dry mouth and urinary retention.

**4.60** Aliphatic compounds are high potency.

**4.61** Although different social classes may have different financial incomes, this is balanced by different levels of happiness, so that all social classes are equal, when everything is taken into account.

**4.62** Aphasia is described as anomic when it does not fit well into any of the defined categories.

**4.63** Lilliputian hallucinations can involve people, animals or inanimate objects.

**4.64** Ambitendence is a form of ambivalence.

**4.65** Reflex hallucinations are commonly experienced on waking.

**4.66** 5-Hydroxytryptamine is metabolised to 5-hydroxytryptophan.

**4.67** Anxiety and fear are mediated by the locus caeruleus.

**4.68** Damage deep inside the left temporal lobe may cause right homonymous upper quadrant visual field defects and a mild right-sided hemiparesis.

**4.69** Presynaptic inhibition characteristically occurs via axon–axonic synapses.

**4.70** The membrane potential of a neurone at rest is approximately – 240 mV.

**4.71**   Benzodiazepines increase β rhythms and decrease α rhythms on the EEG.

**4.72**   Positron emission tomography and single photon emission computed tomography require the injection of radioactive substances to work.

**4.73**   Frontal lobe lesions are associated with spastic paresis because the frontal lobe borders on the motor cortex.

**4.74**   Non-dominant parietal lobe lesions cause constructional apraxia.

**4.75**   Parkinson's disease causes disruption of acetylcholine systems.

**4.76**   People with schizophrenia have a prevalence rate of 15% for tardive dyskinesia, in the absence of drug treatment.

**4.77**   Matched subjects are compared using a t-test.

**4.78**   Ventricular enlargement is irreversible and progressive throughout the lifetime of someone with schizophrenia.

**4.79**   Durkheim described anomie, as a sense of cultural alienation which sometimes contributes to suicide.

**4.80**   The molecular, Purkinje and granular layers are found in the cerebellum.

**4.81**   The correlation between self-reported poor social support and a higher prevalence of depressive symptoms is explained adequately by the idea that depressed people view the world negatively and feel they are unsupported.

**4.82**   Patients respond to the mortification process by colonisation, where they pretend to show acceptance of the institution.

**4.83**   Brains affected by Alzheimer's disease have unusually low levels of aluminium.

**4.84**   Karen Horney described psychosis as a result of repression.

**4.85** Huntington's disease is predominantly subcortical.

**4.86** Double-bind communication is ambiguous.

**4.87** Somatisation rates are culturally determined, to some extent.

**4.88** In terms of significant life events, the death of a spouse is ranked more highly than any other event.

**4.89** Geographical and cultural variation in levels of family support have important implications for provision of psychiatric services.

**4.90** The product–moment correlation coefficient is a sophisticated test that very rarely produces false-positive results.

**4.91** Multiple baseline designs are beneficial because they allow time-lags in interventions, thereby assessing the significance of interventions.

**4.92** Studies using an intention-to-treat analysis are advantageous because they reduce bias which would otherwise occur when dropping out is related to the outcome.

**4.93** Docosahexaenoic acid (DHA) has an important role in development in the fetus and infant.

**4.94** Control subjects should be as different as possible from the subjects under study.

**4.95** Schizophrenia is not more common in those born from July to September in the Southern hemisphere.

**4.96** Cognitive dissonance, described by Festinger, can only truly exist when there is a conflict between attitudes.

**4.97** The revised Wechsler Adult Intelligence Scale (WAIS-R) test consists of 11 subtests.

**4.98** Frustration always leads to aggression.

**4.99**   Pilavin's calculus model applies to bystander intervention, which Latane and Darley classically described as having five stages.

**4.100**   Interval scales are synonymous with ordinal scales.

**4.101**   The primary (or fundamental) attribution error is also known as correspondence bias and results from a tendency to overestimate dispositional rather than situational factors.

**4.102**   Most slow-wave sleep occurs in the first 4 hours.

**4.103**   Attachment is not eradicated by persistent neglect from the attachment figure.

**4.104**   A confident temperament at the age of 3 years is linked to an impulsive personality in early adulthood.

**4.105**   Infants experience a reduction in their fear of heights once they learn to walk.

**4.106**   Larger sibship correlates with decreased intelligence.

**4.107**   Within a family, the oldest child will generally have a higher IQ than the youngest child.

**4.108**   Stranger anxiety usually develops early in the second year of life.

**4.109**   Negative reinforcement, also known as punishment, results from the application of an aversive stimulus.

**4.110**   Photographic memory can be understood as an illusion.

**4.111**   Object constancy, also known as perceptual constancy, incorporates size constancy and occurs at the same time as fear of heights.

**4.112**   Hallucinations are not confined to the mentally ill.

**4.113**   Idiographic personality theories, which are person-centred, are scientifically rigorous because they are based on large-scale studies of populations.

**4.114**  Using repertory grids to measure an individual's personal constructs is often repetitive.

**4.115**  Self-actualisation is achievable by everyone.

**4.116**  Drugs are eliminated in sebum.

**4.117**  The two components of the blood–brain barrier are the cerebral capillary basement membrane and the gliovascular membrane.

**4.118**  Lipid solubility increases the volume of distribution.

**4.119**  Complications of intravenous administration include perivascular necrosis, air embolism and titubation.

**4.120**  Basal ganglia damage causes sensory disorders.

**4.121**  Chlorpromazine was described as inducing 'artificial hibernation'.

**4.122**  Most drugs are metabolised according to zero-order kinetics.

**4.123**  The dominant occipital lobe is usually the site of origin for complex visual hallucinations.

**4.124**  Turner's syndrome is caused by the genotype 45 XO.

**4.125**  Adoption studies are extremely reliable as there are no confounding factors.

**4.126**  Consent should not be assumed and has to be proven by the person giving consent.

**4.127**  The odds ratio is a measure of association.

**4.128**  Doctors should routinely inform the Driver and Vehicle Licensing Authority (DVLA) of deteriorations in a patient's mental state.

**4.129** Most psychotropic drugs were initially identified as clinically useful based on a sophisticated understanding of their clinical properties, based on predictions made from their chemical structure.

**4.130** Kline was influential in early reports of monoamine oxidase efficacy in depressive disorders.

**4.131** Trazodone is a triazolopyridine.

**4.132** Unlike the anterior lobe, the posterior lobe of the pituitary only produces two hormones.

**4.133** Alpha rhythms are characteristically seen in the motor cortex, on motor activity.

**4.134** Once a patient has signed a consent form, they cannot change their mind.

**4.135** The central limit theorem dictates that increasing the size of a sample increases the extent to which it tends towards the normal.

**4.136** Sensitivity is defined as the proportion of people without a given condition who are identified as being disease-free by the instrument under study.

**4.137** The first true randomised controlled trial was published by James in 1912.

**4.138** Humanism emphasises the study of groups of individuals to understand people better in scientific terms.

**4.139** In first-order kinetics, the half-life falls with time.

**4.140** Gender dysphoric disorder is associated with Klinefelter's syndrome.

**4.141** The behaviourist view of language views thought as internal speech.

**4.142** Encounter groups use rock and roll to facilitate brief encounter.

**4.143** β-Endorphin is released in response to stress.

**4.144** The equity theory of interpersonal attraction considers the minimax principle important.

**4.145** *Wahnstimmung* is also known as delusional atmosphere.

**4.146** Bowlby considered attachment to be important in all primates.

**4.147** Bonding is strengthened by tactile contact as soon as possible after birth.

**4.148** Conditioning is the establishment of new behaviour by modifying stimulus–response associations.

**4.149** Hall developed five zones of personal space.

**4.150** Heinroth described hebephrenia in 1871.

**4.151** Infants can mimic adult facial expressions at 36 hours.

**4.152** The concordance for heredity of intelligence of monozygous twins reared apart is 0.70.

**4.153** Tom Main first used the term therapeutic community in 1846.

**4.154** Mirtazepine reduces rapid eye movement sleep and acts as a presynaptic $\alpha_2$-antagonist.

**4.155** Transitional objects help with separation-individuation.

**4.156** Cattell used oblique factor analysis in his study of personality.

**4.157** Concepts of self-psychology are unhelpful when working with narcissists.

**4.158** Balloon cells are seen in Pick's disease.

**4.159**   Babbling occurs only in babies with some degree of hearing.

**4.160**   Bruner described the topic–comment structure of language.

**4.161**   Common group tension describes the difficulties that arise in a group where people have different aims and ideals.

**4.162**   Coprolalia involves ingestion of faeces.

**4.163**   Neglect dyslexia is increased in the presence of distracting stimuli.

**4.164**   Cohort studies enable more accurate measurement of incidence than ecological studies.

**4.165**   Administration of a benzodiazepine characteristically reduces beta rhythms.

# EXTENDED MATCHING ITEMS

## 4.166 THEME: PERSONALITY THEORIES

| | |
|---|---|
| A | Abraham Maslow |
| B | Carl Rogers |
| C | Emile Durkheim |
| D | Fritz Perls |
| E | George Kelly |
| F | Gordon Allport |
| G | Hans Eysenck |
| H | Melanie Klein |
| I | Noam Chomsky |
| J | Sigmund Freud |

**Choose the most appropriate name from the list above for each of the following descriptions.**

1    Described neuroticism as arising from incongruence between the perceived self and the ideal self.

2    Developed personal construct theory, suggesting that people test out their own hypotheses about the world in an attempt to understand it.

3    Used orthogonal factor analysis on soldiers to describe personality on two scales.

## 4.167 THEME: INTRODUCTION OF DRUGS INTO CLINICAL USE

| | |
|---|---|
| A | Brown and Harris |
| B | Cade |
| C | Charpentier |
| D | Delay and Deniker |
| E | Janssen |
| F | Johnson |
| G | Kane |
| H | Laborit |
| I | Lidz |
| J | Paraie and Sigwald |

**Choose the person from the list above who was most instrumental in the introduction into clinical use of each of the following:**

1    Lithium
2    Haloperidol
3    Clozapine.

## 4.168 THEME: NAMES AND IDEAS

| | |
|---|---|
| A | Andresen |
| B | Benjamin Spock |
| C | Fritz Perls |
| D | Fromm-Reichmann |
| E | George Kelly |
| F | Kohut |
| G | Main and Solomon |
| H | Sigmund Freud |
| I | Szasz |
| J | Wynn and Singer |

**Select the name from the list above most closely associated with each of the following ideas:**

1      The schizophrenogenic mother.
2      Type D attachment behaviour – disorganised/disoriented.
3      Positive and negative symptoms of schizophrenia.

## 4.169   THEME: RADIOLIGANDS

| | |
|---|---|
| A | $^{11}$C-carfentanil |
| B | $^{11}$C-DOPA |
| C | $^{14}$C-DOPA |
| D | $^{11}$C-fallypride |
| E | $^{17}$C-FLB 457 |
| F | $^{11}$C-flumazenil |
| G | $^{11}$C-raclopride |
| H | $^{123}$I-IBZM |
| I | $^{123}$I-ICBM |
| J | $^{123}$I-iomazenil |

This is a subject which may not have been covered in revision but which has been tested recently in the actual examination.

**Identify the most appropriate radioligand from the list above for the investigation of each of the following:**

1   Dopamine turnover examined by positron emission tomography.
2   Dopamine D2 receptor binding measured by single photon emission computed tomography.
3   γ-Aminobutyric acid (GABA)–benzodiazepine receptor binding measured by positron emission tomography.

### 4.170   THEME: FEARS

| | |
|---|---|
| A | Animals |
| B | Burglary |
| C | Death |
| D | Failing examinations |
| E | Failure |
| F | Monsters |
| G | Social shame |
| H | Strangers |
| I | The dark |
| J | The number 13 |

**For each of the following ages, identify the most likely source of fear from the list above.**

| | |
|---|---|
| 1 | 8 years |
| 2 | 8 months |
| 3 | 80 years. |

## 4.171   THEME: GENDER DIFFERENCES IN PSYCHIATRIC DISORDERS

| | |
|---|---|
| A | Alcohol abuse |
| B | Anorexia nervosa |
| C | Bipolar disorder |
| D | Histrionic personality disorder |
| E | Paraphilias |
| F | Schizoaffective disorder |
| G | Schizophrenia |
| H | Schizophrenia of onset age 40 years or older |
| I | Tourette's syndrome |

**Choose the three disorders from the above list which correspond to each of the following:**

1   More common in men.
2   More common in women.
3   No gender difference.

## 4.172 THEME: THE HISTORY OF SCHIZOPHRENIA

| | |
|---|---|
| A | Ambitendence |
| B | Catatonia |
| C | Demence precoce |
| D | Dementia praecox |
| E | Expressed emotion |
| F | First-rank symptoms |
| G | Gegenhalten |
| H | Hebephrenia |
| I | Research Diagnostic Criteria (RDC) |
| J | Social labelling theory |

**Identify the concept from the list above most closely associated with each of the following names:**

1 Kahlbaum
2 Kurt Schneider
3 Hecker
4 Morel
5 Spitzer
6 Kraepelin.

## 4.173 THEME: RADIOLIGANDS

| | |
|---|---|
| A | ¹¹C-carfentanil |
| B | ¹¹C-diprenorphine |
| C | ¹¹C-DOPA |
| D | ¹²³I-epidepride |
| E | ¹¹C-fallypride |
| F | ¹¹C-flumazenil |
| G | ¹¹C-SCH 23390 |
| H | ¹²³I-IBZM |
| I | ¹²³I-FP-CIT |
| J | ¹²³I-iomazenil |

**Choose the appropriate radioligand from the list above for each of the following investigations:**

1     Positron emission tomography assessment of γ-aminobutyric acid–benzodiazepine receptors.
2     Single photon emission computed tomography assessment of extrastriatal D2 receptors.
3     Positron emission tomography examination of D1 receptors.
4     Single photon emission computed tomography assessment of γ-aminobutyric acid–benzodiazepine receptors.

## 4.174   THEME: ANTIPSYCHOTIC CLASSIFICATION

| | |
|---|---|
| A | Benzisothiazole |
| B | Benzixasole |
| C | Butyrophenon |
| D | Dibenzothiazepinee |
| E | Piperazine |
| F | Piperidine |
| G | Quinolinone |
| H | Substituted benzamide |
| I | Thienobenzodiazepine |
| J | Thioxanthine |

Choose the classification from the list above for each of the following antipsychotics:

1   Aripiprazole
2   Zuclopenthixol
3   Olanzapine
4   Quetiapine.

# PRACTICE PAPER 4

## Answers

### INDIVIDUAL STATEMENT QUESTIONS

**4.1** **True**

**4.2** **True**

**4.3** **True**
Fear p117–18

**4.4** **False** – It is pulsatile and highly variable.

**4.5** **True**

**4.6** **False** – They often provide negative feedback, inhibiting release of the neurotransmitter.

**4.7** **True** – They have low social and cognitive competencies, and can be aggressive.

**4.8** **True** – Common fears at this age also include animals, the dark and loud noises.
A–Z p144–5

**4.9** **True** – This idea was described by Erikson in his final stage (late adulthood) of integrity versus despair.
A–Z p138–9

**4.10** **False** – There is no evidence to support this.

**4.11** **False** – Olsen described the circumflex model of the family.

**4.12** **True** – It is a statistical term used in this sense.

**4.13** **False** – They are used to analyse samples, so they are inferential.

**4.14**   **False** – It was described by Kurt Schneider, along with other first- and second-rank symptoms of schizophrenia. Carl Schneider described substitution, derailment, drivelling, fusion and omission.

**4.15**   **True** – In some elderly people, there may be no short-wave sleep at all during a night's sleep.

**4.16**   **False** – $\alpha_1$-receptors are post-synaptic and $\alpha_2$-receptors are presynaptic.
Fear p154

**4.17**   **True** – It is the main excitatory neurotransmitter, and has a central role in reward, pleasure and addiction.

**4.18**   **False** – The NMDA receptor is an ionotropic glutamate receptor.
Fear p152–3

**4.19**   **True**

**4.20**   **False** – Sex hormones are not important in determining the style of parenting.
A–Z p240

**4.21**   **True** – 'Responsive parenting' occurs when parents adapt to their child's needs.
Fear p50

**4.22**   **True** – They are the D1-like receptors. D2, D3 and D4 are the D2-like receptors.
Fear p155

**4.23**   **True**

**4.24**   **True**

**4.25**   **True**

**4.26**   **False** – Suppression produces hunger; it is stimulation that produces satiety.

**4.27** **True**
A–Z p192

**4.28** **False** – It inhibits thyroid-stimulating hormone (TSH) production. TSH production is increased by thyrotrophin-releasing hormone.

**4.29** **False** – Fine tremor is seen at therapeutic doses. Coarse tremor is seen only at toxic doses and is a sign of potentially life-threatening toxicity.

**4.30** **False** – There is another stage, bargaining, between anger and depression.

**4.31** **True** – Many of his ideas about the effect of culture on health are valid in a range of contexts.

**4.32** **True**

**4.33** **True** – Enacted stigma results when discrimination occurs. Felt stigma is the fear of enacted stigma.

**4.34** **True** – This is seen currently in Western Europe where the population is ageing, with important implications for psychiatric services.

**4.35** **True** – There are five groups of symptoms: somatic distress, sleep disturbance, movement disorders, behavioural activation and miscellaneous symptoms.

**4.36** **True**

**4.37** **False** – It increases side-effects and minimises therapeutic effects.

**4.38** **False** – It is the antagonism here which causes extrapyramidal side-effects.

**4.39** **False** – St John's Wort has effects similar to those of prescribed antidepressants.

**4.40**   **True**
Fear p156

**4.41**   **True** – Also the form and solubility of the drug, the p*K*a and the blood flow through the area of administration.

**4.42**   **False** – Only tRNA.

**4.43**   **False** – Groupthink is the tendency of groups to act as a single cohesive unit and reach decisions by putting aside differing opinions. It is more prominent with a lack of time and a strong leader.
A–Z p157

**4.44**   **True** – Alcohol has direct effects on fetal development and can lead to fetal alcohol syndrome. There is a dose–response effect and even low levels can cause behavioural changes in the child.

**4.45**   **True** – However, only a small percentage of cases are caused by this. Most result from trisomy 21 following non-disjunction.

**4.46**   **False**

**4.47**   **False** – One in four.

**4.48**   **True**

**4.49**   **False** – It is a disorder of carbohydrate metabolism.

**4.50**   **False** – It is autosomal dominant.

**4.51**   **False** – Magnetic resonance imaging has a resolution of 1 mm, single photon emission computed tomography has a resolution of 8 mm.

**4.52**   **True** – Larger fibres increase transmission speed.

**4.53**   **True** – Non-rapid eye movement (REM) sleep is controlled by serotonergic neurones in the raphe nucleus and REM sleep by noradrenergic neurones in the locus caeruleus.

**4.54** **True** – These abnormalities are characterised by delay in the evoked potential and are also seen in relatives of those with schizophrenia.

**4.55** **False** – There are 46, which includes the sex chromosomes.

**4.56** **True**

**4.57** **False** – They are type I.

**4.58** **True** – Although these areas are poorly localised.

**4.59** **False** – The effect is peripheral rather than central. Constipation and blurred vision also result.

**4.60** **False** – Low potency.

**4.61** **False** – Social classes result from inequality.

**4.62** **False** – It is the inability to name objects, also known as nominal aphasia.

**4.63** **False** – They involve people or animals.

**4.64** **True** – It occurs when an initial movement in one direction is reversed and occurs in the opposite direction.

**4.65** **False** – Hypnopompic hallucinations are experienced on waking. Reflex hallucinations are described as occurring in one modality in response to a stimulus in a different modality.

**4.66** **False** – 5-Hydroxytryptophan is metabolised to 5-hydroxytryptamine (serotonin).

**4.67** **True**

**4.68** **True**

**4.69** **True**

**4.70** **False** – It is approximately -70 mV.
Fear p139

**4.71** **True**

**4.72** **True**

**4.73** **True**

**4.74** **True** – They also cause topographical apraxia.

**4.75** **True**

**4.76** **True**

**4.77** **True**

**4.78** **False** – It is irreversible but not usually progressive.

**4.79** **True** – Durkheim described anomie in his book *The Division of Labour in Society*, as occurring when society becomes deregulated to the extent that people do not know what to expect from one another and become confused about their roles.

**4.80** **True** – These are the three cerebellar layers.
A–Z p72, Fear p120–2

**4.81** **False** – This is unlikely. There is more evidence to suggest that low levels of social support lead to higher rates of depressive symptoms.

**4.82** **True**

**4.83** **False** – Aluminium levels are usually higher than normal.

**4.84** **True**
A–Z p167

**4.85** **True** – The subcortical dementias include Parkinson's disease and Huntington's disease.

A–Z p98

**4.86**   **True** – It was described by Bateson as a risk factor for schizophrenia.

**4.87**   **True**

**4.88**   **True**

**4.89**   **True**

**4.90**   **False** – It frequently produces false-positive results, even when the two rating mechanisms it is comparing actually have a low correlation. It is sensitive to chance agreement in ratings.

**4.91**   **True**

**4.92**   **True** – Other advantages include guarding against attempts to influence the results by excluding unusual outcomes, preserving the baseline comparability between the groups and ignoring adherence in analysing results, thereby giving a more accurate indication of how the treatment will perform in reality.

**4.93**   **True** – It is provided by the mother prior to birth and synthesised by the infant after birth. It is implicated in ocular and cerebral development.

**4.94**   **False** – They should be as similar as possible, with the exception of the variable being studied.

**4.95**   **False** – It is up to 10% more common then than in other months, because these are winter births.

**4.96**   **False** – There can be a conflict between thoughts, beliefs and attitudes.
A–Z p119

**4.97**   **True** – It is divided into verbal and performance tasks.

**4.98**   **False** – This was a theory put forward by Dollard and Miller, but it is not true in all cases. Questions featuring the word

'always' are usually, but not always, false.
Fear p39

**4.99** **True** – The stages are awareness, emotional arousal, interpretation, cost–benefit analysis and decision.
A–Z p68, Fear p40–2

**4.100** **False** – Ordinal scales measure along a continuum and by definition specify the relationship between different points on a scale, whereas interval scales measure according to discrete points.
Fear p64

**4.101** **True**
See A–Z p52, Fear p32

**4.102** **True** – Slow-wave sleep (stages 3 and 4) occurs early in the night.

**4.103** **True** – Attachment will be affected by abuse or neglect from the attachment figure, but will occur nonetheless.
A–Z p46–7

**4.104** **True**
A–Z p317

**4.105** **False** – Fear of heights increases when a child learns to walk.
A–Z p144–5

**4.106** **True** – Only children undergo slightly more rapid intellectual development and children born to larger families have slightly lower IQs.
A–Z p144

**4.107** **True**

**4.108** **False** – It develops from 6 months of age, but reaches its peak at 18 months to 2 years, before diminishing.

**4.109** **False** – The difference between negative reinforcement and punishment is that the aversive stimulus is applied after the

behaviour in punishment. In negative reinforcement, the aversive stimulus is present initially and can be removed by good behaviour.
A–Z p81, Fear p5–6

**4.110** **False** – Images in photographic memory are not seen as perceptions, so this is not an illusory or hallucinatory experience.
A–Z p208

**4.111** **False** – Object constancy develops gradually between the ages of 3 and 10 years. Fear of heights is well developed by the time a child is crawling, usually in their first year of life.

**4.112** **True** – Hallucinations can occur in people without mental illness. An example would be seeing fleeting glimpses of a recently deceased person.

**4.113** **False** – Idiographic personality theories are person centred, but are based on individual case studies. They emphasise individual experience and the uniqueness of individuals rather than scientific theories which make generalisations.

**4.114** **True** – Repertory grids compare many different elements of a person's life (people, places, concepts, etc) in terms of the person's affect towards them. This is repeated for many different aspects of their life to build up an understanding of how they view the world and their place in it.

**4.115** **True** – According to Maslow, self-actualisation, at the top of his hierarchy of needs, is achievable by everyone in theory, although few people achieve it in practice.
A–Z p203

**4.116** **True**
A–Z p132

**4.117** **False** – The third component is the tight junctions between capillary endothelial cells.

**4.118** **True**
A–Z p120–2

**4.119** **False** – Titubation is the nodding of the head as a result of illness, such as multiple sclerosis.

**4.120** **False** – The basal ganglia have predominantly a motor function.

**4.121** **True**

**4.122** **False** – Zero-order kinetics are independent of the amount of the drug present. The most common example is alcohol, when the processing enzymes are saturated.
Fear p145

**4.123** **False** – It is the non-dominant lobe.

**4.124** **True**

**4.125** **False** – Non-random adoption causes bias.

**4.126** **False** – Ability to consent should be assumed in all cases, unless proven otherwise.

**4.127** **True**

**4.128** **False** – Doctors should advise patients that they may not be fit to drive and encourage them to inform the Driver and Vehicle Licensing Authority (DVLA).

**4.129** **False** – Most were discovered by chance while being tested for use in other circumstances.

**4.130** **True**

**4.131** **True**

**4.132** **True** – Antidiuretic hormone and oxytocin.

**4.133** **False** – This describes mu rhythms. Alpha rhythms are seen

with the eyes closed in low states of arousal.
A–Z p365

**4.134**  **False** – Consent can be given or retracted at any time.

**4.135**  **True**

**4.136**  **False** – Sensitivity is the proportion of people with the condition who test positive for it.

**4.137**  **False** – It was published by Hill in 1952.

**4.138**  **False** – It emphasises individual experience and does not value the scientific method as an appropriate means of studying individuals.

**4.139**  **False** – This is not necessarily the case, but can be seen when enzymes are induced by the drug.
Fear p145.

**4.140**  **True**

**4.141**  **True**
A–Z p191

**4.142**  **False** – They use rocking and rolling to facilitate basic encounter.

**4.143**  **True**
A–Z p135

**4.144**  **True** – This is the maximisation of reward and minimisation of cost in interpersonal interactions.

**4.145**  **True**

**4.146**  **False** – Only in higher primates.

**4.147**  **True**

**4.148**  **True**

**4.149**   **False** – Only four zones.

**4.150**   **False** – Heinroth described *verruckheit*. Hecker described hebephrenia in 1871.

**4.151**   **True**
A–Z p178

**4.152**   **True** – When reared together, it increases to 0.85.

**4.153**   **False** – It was used in 1946.

**4.154**   **True**

**4.155**   **True**

**4.156**   **True**

**4.157**   **False**

**4.158**   **True**

**4.159**   **False** – It also occurs in babies with no hearing at all.

**4.160**   **True**
A–Z p65–6

**4.161**   **False** – It was described by Ezriel as the conflict arising in therapeutic relationships as a result of a shared longing for an inappropriate relationship between therapist and patient.

**4.162**   **False** – This is coprophilia. Coprolalia is the use of obscene language.

**4.163**   **True** – This is mistaking one word for another as a result of inattention.

**4.164**   **True**

**4.165**   **False** – Anxiolytics increase beta rhythms. Antidepressants and antipsychotics cause a reduction.

# EXTENDED MATCHING ITEMS

## 4.166 THEME: PERSONALITY THEORIES

1    **B** – Carl Rogers
2    **E** – George Kelly
3    **G** – Hans Eysenck
A–Z p247–51

## 4.167 THEME: INTRODUCTION OF DRUGS INTO CLINICAL USE

1    **B** – Cade. Lange first suggested its use in 1886
2    **E** – Janssen
3    **G** – Kane – conducted trials which led to the reintroduction of clozapine after it was initially withdrawn

## 4.168 THEME: NAMES AND IDEAS

1    **D** – Fromm-Reichmann
2    **G** – Main and Solomon
3    **A** – Andresen

## 4.169 THEME: RADIOLIGANDS

1    **B** – $^{11}$C-DOPA
2    **H** – $^{123}$I-IBZM
3    **F** – $^{11}$C-flumazenil
Fear p174–5

## 4.170 THEME: FEARS

1    **G** – Social shame
2    **H** – Strangers
3    **B** – Burglary

## 4.171 THEME: GENDER DIFFERENCES IN PSYCHIATRIC DISORDERS

1    **A, E, I** – Alcohol abuse, Paraphilias and Tourette's syndrome

2        **B, F, H** – Anorexia nervosa, Schizoaffective disorder and
         Schizophrenia of onset age 40 years or older
3        **C, D, G** – Bipolar disorder, Histrionic personality disorder
         and Schizophrenia

### 4.172   THEME: THE HISTORY OF SCHIZOPHRENIA

1        **B** – Catatonia
2        **F** – First-rank symtoms
3        **H** – Hebephrenia
4        **C** – Demence precoce
5        **I** – Research Diagnostic Criteria (RDC)
6        **D** – Dementia praecox
Fear p222

### 4.173   THEME: RADIOLIGANDS

1        **F** – $^{11}$C-flumazenil
2        **D** – $^{123}$I-epidepride
3        **G** – $^{11}$C-SCH 23390
4        **J** – $^{123}$I-iomazenil
Fear p175

### 4.174   THEME: ANTIPSYCHOTIC CLASSIFICATION

1        **G** – Quinolinone
2        **J** – Thioxanthine
3        **I** – Thienobenzodiazepine
4        **D** – Dibenzothiazepine

# CLINICAL SCIENCES
PRACTICE PAPERS

# PRACTICE PAPER 5

*Time allowed: 90 minutes*

## INDIVIDUAL STATEMENT QUESTIONS

**5.1** People with bulimia nervosa have a morbid fear of fatness and a desire to maintain their weight below their ideal weight.

**5.2** The difference in age between an elderly patient undergoing dynamic psychotherapy and the therapist may be problematic.

**5.3** Future excessive use of alcohol can be predicted by close examination of the mother–child relationship at 1 year.

**5.4** Encephalopathy associated with beri-beri presents in a manner similar to Wernicke's encephalopathy.

**5.5** Heroin is also known as 'horse'.

**5.6** Primary enuresis has a better prognosis than secondary enuresis.

**5.7** Compulsions are often seen in children with autism.

**5.8** Many arsonists are under 15 years of age.

**5.9** Cognitive behavioural therapy examines childhood to understand the present.

**5.10** Lesch–Nyhan syndrome involves excess production of uric acid and is associated with the scissor position of the arms.

**5.11** HIV dementia commonly presents with apathy.

**5.12** Chaining is useful in learning difficulties.

**5.13** Most people with an IQ of 35–49 can still manage to live independently.

**5.14** Attention deficit hyperactivity disorder (ADHD) is more commonly diagnosed in France than in the United States.

**5.15** The prevalence of depressive disorder in people committing suicide is less than 50%.

**5.16** Victims of infanticide must be aged between 6 months and 2 years.

**5.17** More than 90% of prisoners in the United Kingdom have substance-misuse problems.

**5.18** Most abnormal homicides result from automatisms.

**5.19** Concordance for criminality is almost five times higher in monozygotic than dizygotic twins.

**5.20** At the start of an interview in a child psychiatry clinic, toys should be tipped onto the floor.

**5.21** Common law is also known as judge-made law.

**5.22** The corpus callosum is affected in Patau's syndrome.

**5.23** Selective positive reinforcement is used in cognitive behavioural therapy.

**5.24** Chronic physical illness in children is associated with parental marital disputes.

**5.25** Postnatal depression is seen in 50% of mothers.

**5.26** Gilles de la Tourette's syndrome characteristically involves emotional difficulties and social problems.

**5.27** Temporal lobe epilepsy can present with forced thinking.

**5.28** Hyperkinetic disorders characteristically present after the 7th year of life.

**5.29** Enuretic children often have physical abnormalities of their bladders.

**5.30** Hysterical disorders only occur in women.

**5.31** Dysmorphophobia is characterised by overvalued ideas but never delusions.

**5.32** Being the eldest child in a family protects against school refusal.

**5.33** Persistent delusional disorder is characterised by encapsulated, bizarre delusions with relative preservation of social functions.

**5.34** A common cause of night terrors is a separation from a partner.

**5.35** Depersonalisation is associated with anxiety.

**5.36** School refusal is more common in males than females.

**5.37** Admission to hospital may exacerbate Lewy body dementia.

**5.38** Obsessive traits always help to increase standards of work.

**5.39** Simple schizophrenia involves prominent positive symptoms with relative preservation of personality.

**5.40** Alzheimer's disease is more likely than Pick's disease if personality deteriorated before memory.

**5.41** In completing the Edinburgh Postnatal Depression Scale, the mother is required to seek the opinions of other family members.

**5.42** There is an association between alcohol use and unplanned pregnancies.

**5.43** Risk factors for hypochondriasis include low social class.

**5.44** Most patients with schizophrenia experience prominent thought disorder.

**5.45** Visual impairment is a risk factor for the development of delusional disorders in elderly populations.

**5.46** Normal pressure hydrocephalus usually affects children.

**5.47** Gender dysphoric disorder is associated with Klinefelter's syndrome.

**5.48** Subarachnoid haemorrhage causes neck stiffness.

**5.49** Aspartate transaminase (AST) is suitable for use as a screening test for alcohol dependence in medical inpatients.

**5.50** Fertility is reduced in very-late-onset schizophrenia.

**5.51** Cerebrovascular accident is a risk factor for depressive disorders in the elderly.

**5.52** Memory disturbance in early Alzheimer's disease is episodic.

**5.53** Methylphenidate is used in the treatment of narcolepsy.

**5.54** Paraphrenia is more common in people with sensory impairment.

**5.55** Relapses of mania are more common in spring than at other times of the year.

**5.56** Problems with separation and independence are associated with anorexia nervosa.

**5.57** Post-traumatic stress disorder involves autonomic signs of severe anxiety.

**5.58** Postnatal blues are associated with hypercalcaemia.

**5.59** Child abuse can lead to neonatal maternal separation.

**5.60** Piblokto is seen in Inuit women and relates to childbirth.

**5.61** Normal syntactic structure is maintained more commonly in mania than in schizophrenia.

**5.62** An inquisitorial system is used in common law jurisdictions.

**5.63** The clinical effects of disulfiram can be seen after very small amounts of alcohol are consumed.

**5.64** Khat can cause bipolar affective disorder.

**5.65** Alcohol detoxification should be carried out with disulfiram and chlordiazepoxide in most cases.

**5.66** Delirium tremens is usually self-limiting and can safely be managed at home.

**5.67** Substance misuse is a risk factor for violent offending in schizophrenia.

**5.68** Mannerisms are goal-directed.

**5.69** Risk factors for depressive disorders in the elderly include genetic factors and Parkinson's disease.

**5.70** Mean survival in Edward's syndrome is 4–5 years.

**5.71** Cognitive therapy involves collaborative empiricism, which involves placing blind faith in the therapist.

**5.72** Therapeutic communities work by acting through the group.

**5.73** Self-harm in Lesch–Nyhan syndrome is generally limited to nail-biting.

**5.74** Fifty per cent of children with autism never develop spoken language.

**5.75** Low IQ is associated with conduct disorder in childhood.

**5.76** Hypertension is an independent risk factor for the development of both vascular dementia and Alzheimer's disease.

**5.77** Old age is a risk factor for the development of tardive dyskinesia.

**5.78** Diogenes syndrome is more common in males than females.

**5.79** Alzheimer's disease presents early in Down's syndrome, usually before the age of 55 years.

**5.80** Restlessness is more suggestive of delirium than dementia.

**5.81** Tuberous sclerosis is strongly associated with seizures and hamartomas in the brain and spinal cord.

**5.82** Obsessive-compulsive disorder has an equal sex incidence.

**5.83** Hebephrenic schizophrenia is more common in highly developed countries.

**5.84** A child who has both parents affected by schizophrenia is overwhelmingly likely to be affected by the same disorder.

**5.85** Huntington's disease causes exaggeration of the EEG.

**5.86** Comorbid depression indicates a poorer prognosis in patients with myocardial infarction.

**5.87** Lewy body dementia is characterised by fluctuating impairment of memory and higher functions.

**5.88** Systemic therapy in the elderly is difficult as they have few involved family members and are usually isolated from social systems.

**5.89** Mental retardation is more common in females.

**5.90** Acquisitive offending is more common in people with learning disability.

**5.91** Gender stability is acquired before gender identity.

**5.92** Lesions associated with Wernicke's encephalopathy are seen in the anterior lobe of the cerebellum.

**5.93** LSD is properly known as lysergic acid dihydride.

**5.94** Hyperkinesis involves excitability, overactivity and impulsivity.

**5.95** Functional analysis of behaviour always forms part of behaviour therapy.

**5.96** If a patient is late for a session of psychoanalytic psychotherapy, the therapy should be ended.

**5.97** Incongruity of affect is a positive symptom of schizophrenia.

**5.98** Dopamine concentrations are decreased in Huntington's disease.

**5.99** Absence seizures are characteristically preceded by an aura.

**5.100** Deliberate self-harm in the elderly is more significant than in a younger population.

**5.101** School refusal is more commonly a problem at the age of 5 than at the age of 11.

**5.102** Speech comprehension is preserved in infantile autism.

**5.103** Tinnitus is associated with benzodiazepine withdrawal.

**5.104** Anorexia nervosa involves a distortion of body image with a dread of fatness presenting as an intrusive delusional idea.

**5.105** A diagnosis of dementia causes testamentary incapacity.

**5.106** Schizophrenia is negatively associated with rheumatoid arthritis.

**5.107** Patients with anorexia nervosa are generally more socially competent than patients with bulimia nervosa.

**5.108** Anhedonia prevents the experience of pleasure and results in a state which is free from affect.

**5.109** Post-traumatic stress disorder causes autonomic signs of severe anxiety.

**5.110** Pseudodementia is associated with a past history of bipolar affective disorder.

**5.111** Alcoholic hallucinosis characteristically occurs in a state of impaired or clouded consciousness.

**5.112** Excessive use of procyclidine can lead to visual hallucinations.

**5.113** Coprolalia is an example of a vocal tic.

**5.114** Stealing from shops is more common in girls than boys, because of its association with depressive disorders.

**5.115** Shoplifting has an association with depressive disorder.

**5.116** Offending rates increase as severity of learning disability increases.

**5.117** Most males with fragile X syndrome have micro-orchidism.

**5.118** Figures from childhood have a significant influence on transference.

**5.119** Ventilation forms part of supportive psychotherapy.

**5.120** Eye movement desensitisation has been demonstrated to be effective in post-traumatic stress disorder.

**5.121** First-degree relatives of people with unipolar depressive disorders are at significantly increased risk of developing bipolar disorder.

**5.122** Russell's sign is seen in anorexia nervosa.

**5.123** Echolalia is a feature of schizophrenia.

**5.124**   Flooding is a rapid process causing great anxiety.

**5.125**   Delusions of passivity are second-rank symptoms of schizophrenia.

**5.126**   A person who cannot understand the evidence against them may still be fit to plead in certain circumstances.

**5.127**   Restlessness, fear and hypersomnia are features of post-partum psychosis.

**5.128**   Night terrors typically occur in stages 2 and 3 of sleep.

**5.129**   IQ is often 60–70 in children with autism.

**5.130**   Normal homicides include those committed during a jealous rage.

**5.131**   Brachycephaly is associated with learning difficulty.

**5.132**   Munchausen syndrome correlates strongly with opiate addiction.

**5.133**   Down's syndrome is protective against Alzheimer's disease.

**5.134**   Psilocybin is more potent than LSD (lysergic acid diethylamide).

**5.135**   There is an association between religious prohibitions on alcohol use and actual use of alcohol.

**5.136**   Epileptiform activity in Creutzfeldt–Jakob disease includes myoclonic jerks.

**5.137**   Munchausen' syndrome has a good overall prognosis.

**5.138**   Dementia is characteristically preceded by delusional disorder.

**5.139**   The typical violent offender is a male in his late 20s.

**5.140**   Psychodrama is potentially a very powerful and direct form of therapy.

**5.141** People with autism never make direct eye contact.

**5.142** Tolerance to amphetamines can result in higher doses being used over time.

**5.143** Action follows contemplation in the stages of change model of addiction.

**5.144** Akathisia is usually seen as a feature of tardive dyskinesia.

**5.145** Gonorrhoea can lead to the development of an Argyll Robertson pupil.

**5.146** Night terrors and nightmares are characterised by a clear memory for the source of the distress when the child wakes.

**5.147** Acute intermittent porphyria is characterised by autosomal dominant inheritance with complete penetrance.

**5.148** Functional analysis examines stimuli which cause behaviours.

**5.149** Lucid intervals suggest a diagnosis of pseudodementia rather than dementia.

**5.150** There is a family history in 20% of cases of frontotemporal dementia.

**5.151** Stimulants may reduce hyperactivity in attention deficit hyperactivity disorder (ADHD).

**5.152** Intellectual disability in Down syndrome becomes apparent in the second year of life.

**5.153** Early deterioration of cortical associative functioning is seen in normal pressure hydrocephalus.

**5.154** Friedreich's ataxia usually causes death from respiratory insufficiency.

**5.155** The pattern of luteinising hormone secretion in anorexia nervosa is similar to that seen pre-pubertally.

**5.156** Characteristic features of generalised anxiety disorder include late insomnia and night terrors.

**5.157** Obsessive-compulsive disorder is associated with anankastic personality disorder in up to 30% of cases.

**5.158** The Hachinski score is used to differentiate vascular and Alzheimer's dementia.

**5.159** Benzodiazepines can cause excessive weight gain.

**5.160** Insecure attachment can contribute to challenging behaviour.

**5.161** Young children usually injure themselves, rather than others, during temper tantrums.

**5.162** Offenders with IQs below 100 are more likely to be caught.

**5.163** Childhood autism characteristically presents between the ages of 3 and 5 years.

**5.164** Increasing incidence of challenging behaviour correlates with increasing severity of learning difficulty.

**5.165** Family relationships are seen as circular.

# EXTENDED MATCHING ITEMS

## 5.166   THEME: DRUG COMPLICATIONS IN PREGNANCY

| | |
|---|---|
| A | Auditory and vestibular nerve damage |
| B | Carcinogenic effects reported in animal studies |
| C | Ebstein anomaly |
| D | Intrauterine growth restriction |
| E | Masculinisation of female fetus |
| F | Neonatal bleeding related to hypofibrinaemia |
| G | Neonatal hypothermia, hypotonia and respiratory depression |
| H | Neonatal lethargy, tremor and hypertonia |
| I | Neonatal tachycardia, irritability and muscle spasms |
| J | Possible inhibition of labour |

**Choose the complications from the list above most associated with use of the following in pregnancy:**

| | |
|---|---|
| 1 | Lithium |
| 2 | Sodium valproate |
| 3 | Imipramine |
| 4 | Olanzapine |
| 5 | Benzodiazepines. |

## 5.167 THEME: CLINICAL EFFECTS ON THE EEG

| | |
|---|---|
| A | Decreased theta rhythms |
| B | Flat trace |
| C | Increased alpha rhythms |
| D | Increased beta rhythms |
| E | Increased delta rhythms |
| F | Reduced delta rhythms |
| G | Spikes |
| H | Tented t waves |
| I | Total loss of alpha rhythms |
| J | Waves |

**Choose the EEG changes from the list above characteristically associated with each of the following:**

1   A 50-year-old man with progressive psychiatric and movement disorder who has a positive family history for similar problems.

2   A 34-year-old woman with a long history of alcohol dependence who has recently stopped drinking completely and is experiencing Lilliputian hallucinations.

3   A 23-year-old man with a first episode of psychosis who has recently started treatment.

## 5.168   THEME: APHASIA

A       Anomic aphasia
B       Broca's aphasia
C       Jargon aphasia
D       Transcortical motor aphasia
E       Transcortical sensory aphasia
F       Wernicke's aphasia

**Choose the most appropriate term from the list above for each of the following:**

1       Difficulty with word-finding, especially with naming objects.
2       Phoneme errors occur despite effort to avoid these, with distorted grammar. Normal language comprehension. Sentences cannot be repeated.
3       Fluent speech with many errors and meaningless words despite normal structure. Auditory comprehension is limited. Sentences can be repeated.

## 5.169 THEME: FUNCTIONAL DISORDERS OF SPEECH AND LANGUAGE

| | |
|---|---|
| A | Alogia |
| B | Aphonia |
| C | Coprolalia |
| D | Logoclonia |
| E | Mutism |
| F | Paragrammatism |
| G | Paralogia |
| H | Paraphasia |
| I | Parapraxis |
| J | Schizophasia |

**Choose the most appropriate term from the list above for each of the following:**

1  Repetition of syllables, seen in Parkinsonism.
2  Incorrect sentence construction causing difficulties in communication.
3  Language so disordered that all meaning is lost.
4  Loss of all richness of language.
5  Loss of ability to produce sound needed for language.
6  Unusual sounds becoming incorporated into normal words.

## 5.170   THEME: CLASSIFICATION OF ILLICIT SUBSTANCES

| | |
|---|---|
| A | Barbiturates |
| B | Buprenorphine |
| C | Cannabis |
| D | Creatine |
| E | Hallucinogenic mushrooms growing wild |
| F | Opium |
| G | Oral amphetamines |
| H | Paracetamol |
| I | Phencyclidine |
| J | Solvents |

**Choose two illicit substances from the above list which belong to:**

| | |
|---|---|
| 1 | Class A |
| 2 | Class B |
| 3 | Class C. |

## 5.171 THEME: PERSONALITY DISORDERS

| | |
|---|---|
| A | Anankastic personality disorder |
| B | Anxious personality disorder |
| C | Dependent personality disorder |
| D | Dissocial personality disorder |
| E | Emotionally unstable personality disorder |
| F | Histrionic personality disorder |
| G | Paranoid personality disorder |
| H | Schizoid personality disorder |
| I | Schizotypal personality disorder |

**Choose the personality disorder from the list above most appropriately described by each of the following, according to the International Classifications of Diseases 10th revision (ICD-10):**

1    A distant, somewhat aloof person with little warm interpersonal affect and a preference for scientific and mathematical rather than practical concerns.

2    Eccentric behaviour, magical thinking and pseudohallucinations on a background of little warmth, accompanied by an interest in abstract concepts.

3    Marked subservience and a passive personality style, seeking guidance and direction from others with regard to everyday tasks.

## 5.172   THEME: PSYCHOPATHOLOGY

| | |
|---|---|
| A | Derailment |
| B | Drivelling |
| C | Interpretation |
| D | Metonym |
| E | Omission |
| F | Over-inclusive thinking |
| G | Paragrammatism |
| H | Parapraxis |
| I | Paraphasia |
| J | Substitution |

**Identify the term from the list above for each of the following clinical descriptions:**

1       The breakdown of connections between one thought and another.

2       Extreme formal thought disorder resulting in totally incomprehensible speech.

3       A mistake in speech which causes the speech to have a different meaning to that which was intended and may reveal something about the speaker's attitudes or beliefs which was intended to be kept private.

4       The loss of preservation of conceptual boundaries.

5       Imprecise approximations of words or phrases

# PRACTICE PAPER 5

## Answers

### INDIVIDUAL STATEMENT QUESTIONS

**5.1**    **True** – This is true of both anorexia and bulimia nervosa.
A–Z p66–7

**5.2**    **True** – It may be difficult because of transference but it may
be an advantage.

**5.3**    **False** – There is no such relationship.

**5.4**    **False** – This is the case with pellagra, but not beri-beri.

**5.5**    **True**
Fear p486

**5.6**    **True**
A–Z p135

**5.7**    **True**

A–Z p53

**5.8**    **True** – Offenders are characteristically very young.

Fear p427

**5.9**    **False** – It concentrates on very recent, current and future
situations.

**5.10**   **False** – The scissor position affects the legs.
A–Z p194–5

**5.11**   **True**

**5.12** **True** – This refers to breaking up a task into smaller tasks then teaching these individually.

**5.13** **False**

**5.14** **False** – It is more commonly diagnosed in the United States.

**5.15** **True**
A–Z p310–11

**5.16** **False** – Between 0 and 12 months.

**5.17** **False** – It is less than 70%, although exact rates are difficult to ascertain.

**5.18** **False** – Only a very small proportion.

**5.19** **True**

**5.20** **False** – Toys should be available but not scattered about.

**5.21** **True** – It is made over the years by cases setting precedents. These cases are decided by judges.

**5.22** **True**

**5.23** **False** – It is used in operant therapy.
A–Z p320–1

**5.24** **True**

**5.25** **False** – It is seen in 10–15% of mothers.
A–Z p259–60

**5.26** **False** – It is associated with these, but they are not characteristic.

**5.27** **True** – This is the subjective need to think about a particular subject.
A–Z p137

**5.28**   **False** – They present before the age of 6  years.

**5.29**   **True**

**5.30**   **False**

**5.31**   **False** – It can take the form of a delusion, particularly if it is co-morbid with another psychiatric disorder.
A–Z p127

**5.32**   **True**

**5.33**   **False** – The delusions are non-bizarre.
A–Z p 61, 113–14

**5.34**   **False**

**5.35**   **True** – Anxiety can cause depersonalisation.
A–Z p38–9

**5.36**   **False** – There is equal sex incidence.

**5.37**   **True** – As a result of unfamiliar surroundings and people.

**5.38**   **False** – Excessive obsessionality slows performance.

**5.39**   **False** – It involves a lack of positive symptoms.
A–Z p292

**5.40**   **False** – The reverse is true.
A–Z p256–7

**5.41**   **False** – She should avoid involving others.

**5.42**   **True**

**5.43**   **True**
A–Z p172

**5.44**   **False** – True thought disorder is uncommon.

**5.45**   **True**
Fear p460–1

**5.46**   **False** – Most patients are elderly.
Fear p454

**5.47**   **True**

**5.48**   **True**

**5.49**   **False** – This correlates poorly with alcohol dependence.
$\gamma$-glutamyl transpeptidase  is a much better screening test.

**5.50**   **True**

**5.51**   **True**

**5.52**   **False** – It is semantic.
A–Z p209

**5.53**   **True**

**5.54**   **True**
A–Z p239

**5.55**   **False** – They are more common in summer.
A–Z p8–12

**5.56**   **True**
A–Z p26–9

**5.57**   **False** – It does involve hyperarousal, which is anxiety, but not
severe anxiety.
A–Z p260–3

**5.58**   **False** – Hypocalcaemia.
A–Z p259

**5.59**   **True**

**5.60**   **False** – It relates to food shortages.

**5.61**   **True**

**5.62**   **False** – Common law systems use an adversarial system. Inquisitorial systems are common in systems where there is codified law.

**5.63**   **True** – The alcohol in after-shave can trigger the effects.

**5.64**   **False** – It can produce a mania-like episode or precipitate a manic relapse in bipolar affective disorder.

**5.65**   **False** – Disulfiram is indicated for prevention of relapse. It should never be used in patients who are suspected of having been drinking recently.

**5.66**   **False** – It needs treating as an emergency and has a significant mortality.

**5.67**   **True**

**5.68**   **True**

**5.69**   **True**
Fear p458

**5.70**   **False** – It is often less than 1 year.

**5.71**   **False** – Collaborative empiricism is used in cognitive therapy and cognitive behavioural therapy but it involves testing beliefs in a scientific manner.

**5.72**   **True**

**5.73**   **False** – It is often severe.

**5.74**   **True**

**5.75**   **True**

**5.76**   **True**
Fear p449

**5.77** **True**

**5.78** **False** – The gender incidence is equal.

**5.79** **True**

**5.80** **True**

**5.81** **True**

**5.82** **True** – Overall, this is true, but some subtypes have an unequal sex distribution.
A–Z p230–1

**5.83** **False** – It is more common in less developed countries.
A–Z p281–6

**5.84** **False** – The lifetime incidence is less than 50% in this case.
A–Z p287–91

**5.85** **False** – The EEG is flattened.
A–Z p167–9

**5.86** **True**

**5.87** **True**
A–Z p97–8

**5.88** **False** – This is not true. Carers and residential or nursing home staff can become involved.
Fear p467

**5.89** **False** – It is more common in males.

**5.90** **False** – Only sexual offending.

**5.91** **False** – Gender identity is acquired by 2–3 years. Gender stability is the permanence of gender identity and is acquired by 4 years.

**5.92**   **True**
A–Z p343–6

**5.93**   **False** – Lysergic acid diethylamide.

**5.94**   **True** – Also distractibility.

**5.95**   **True**
A–Z p320

**5.96**   **False** – The therapy should continue, with robust boundaries around the timing of sessions.

**5.97**   **True**
A–Z p281–6

**5.98**   **False** – They are unchanged.
A–Z p167–9

**5.99**   **False**

**5.100**   **True**

**5.101**   **False** – The reverse is true.

**5.102**   **False**
A–Z p53

**5.103**   **True**

**5.104**   **False** – The idea is overvalued rather than delusional.
A–Z p26–9

**5.105**   **False** – Some people with dementia will still be able to make a will.

**5.106**   **True**
A–Z p281–6

**5.107**   **False** – The reverse is true.

A–Z p26–9

**5.108**   **False** – It is unpleasant in itself and results in a state with negative affect.
A–Z p26

**5.109**   **False** – There is anxiety, but it is not severe.
A–Z p260–3

**5.110**   **True**

**5.111**   **False** – It occurs in clear consciousness, by definition.

**5.112**   **True**

**5.113**   **True** – This is the use of obscene language.

**5.114**   **False** – It is not more common in girls than boys and there is very little relationship to depressive disorders in children.

**5.115**   **True** – Low value items are characteristically stolen.

**5.116**   **False** – Mild and moderate learning disability are associated with increases in offending whereas severe learning disability is not.

**5.117**   **False** – Macro-orchidism.

**5.118**   **True**

**5.119**   **True**

**5.120**   **True**

**5.121**   **False**
A–Z p12–14

**5.122**   **True** – It is also seen in bulimia nervosa. 50% of people with anorexia nervosa binge eat.
A–Z p26–9

**5.123**  **True**
A–Z p129

**5.124**  **True**

**5.125**  **False** – They are first-rank symptoms.

**5.126**  **False**

**5.127**  **False** – Insomnia is characteristic, rather than hypersomnia.

**5.128**  **False** – They occur in stages 3 and 4.
A–Z p225

**5.129**  **True** – Although the IQ may be normal.

**5.130**  **True**

**5.131**  **True**

**5.132**  **False**

**5.133**  **False** – It is a risk factor.
A–Z p106–10, Fear p449

**5.134**  **False** – LSD (lysergic acid diethylamide) is much more potent than psilocybin.

**5.135**  **True** – Religious prohibitions are associated with reduced consumption.

**5.136**  **True**
A–Z p110–11

**5.137**  **False** – The prognosis is poor.
A–Z p218–19

**5.138**  **False**

**5.139**  **False** – He is a male aged 18 years.

**5.140** **True** – Which makes it potentially damaging.

**5.141** **False** – The answer to questions featuring the words 'never' and 'always' are (almost) always false. Autism causes great difficulties with eye contact, but it is made, even occasionally.

**5.142** **True**

**5.143** **False** – The stages are precontemplation, contemplation, preparation, action and maintenance. Strictly, preparation (rather than action) follows contemplation. This is an ambiguous question, common in the examination, and can be argued over at length.

**5.144** **False** – It can form part of tardive dyskinesia, but this is unusual.
A–Z p19

**5.145** **False** – It is caused by syphilis.

**5.146** **False** – Night terrors are not remembered.

**5.147** **False** – The penetrance is incomplete.
A–Z p258–9

**5.148** **True**

**5.149** **True**

**5.150** **False** – 50%.
Fear p453

**5.151** **True**

**5.152** **False** – It becomes apparent in the first few months of life.

**5.153** **False** – This is usually preserved.
A–Z p169

**5.154** **False** – Death is usually from cardiac failure.

**5.155** **True**
A–Z p26–9

**5.156** **False** – The insomnia is early. Night terrors are a characteristic feature.
A–Z p114–15

**5.157** **True**
A–Z p230–1

**5.158** **True** – It is used for this but evidence supporting its use is poor.

**5.159** **True**

**5.160** **True**

**5.161** **False** – They rarely injure themselves.

**5.162** **False**

**5.163** **False** – Before 3 years.

**5.164** **True**

**5.165** **True** – This means that the relationships relate to both causes and effects of behaviour within the family.

## EXTENDED MATCHING QUESTIONS

### 5.166 THEME: DRUG COMPLICATIONS IN PREGNANCY

1    **C** – Ebstein anomaly
2    **F** – Neonatal bleeding related to hypofibrinaemia
3    **I** – Neonatal tachycardia, irritability and muscle spasms
4    **H** – Neonatal lethargy, tremor and hypertonia
5    **G** – Neonatal hypothermia, hypotonia and respiratory depression

### 5.167 THEME: CLINICAL EFFECTS ON THE EEG

1    **I** – Total loss of alpha rhythms, as a result of Huntington's disease
2    **D** – Increased beta rhythms, as a result of delirium tremens
3    **E** – Increased delta rhythms, as a result of antipsychotics
     A–Z p365–6

### 5.168 THEME: APHASIA

1    **A** – Anomic aphasia (also known as nominal aphasia)
2    **B** – Broca's aphasia
3    **F** – Wernicke's aphasia
     A–Z p41–2

### 5.169 THEME: FUNCTIONAL DISORDERS OF SPEECH AND LANGUAGE

1    **D** – Logoclonia
2    **F** – Paragrammatism
3    **J** – Schizophasia
4    **A** – Alogia
5    **B** – Aphonia
6    **H** – Paraphasia
     Fear p102

**5.170 THEME: CLASSIFICATION OF ILLICIT SUBSTANCES**

1     **F & I** – Opium and Phencyclidine
2     **A & G** – Barbiturates and Oral amphetamines
3     **B & C** – Buprenorphine and Cannabis

**5.171 THEME: PERSONALITY DISORDERS**

1     **H** – Schizoid personality disorder
2     **I** – Schizotypal personality disorder
3     **C** – Dependent personality disorder

**5.172 THEME: PSYCHOPATHOLOGY**

1     **A** – Derailment
2     **B** – Drivelling
3     **I** – Parapraxis
4     **F** – Over-inclusive thinking
5     **D** – Metonym

# PRACTICE PAPER 6

*Time allowed: 90 minutes*

## INDIVIDUAL STATEMENT QUESTIONS

**6.1** Unusual, progressive, writhing hand movements are a feature of Prader–Willi syndrome.

**6.2** Post-traumatic stress disorder involves intrusive thoughts about the stressful event, but difficulty recalling it voluntarily.

**6.3** Abulia is a negative symptom of schizophrenia.

**6.4** Anomic aphasia leads to circumlocutions.

**6.5** Semantic memory disturbance is seen in herpes simplex virus encephalitis.

**6.6** Visual hallucinations in Bonnet's syndrome are typically monochrome.

**6.7** Cannabis is often injected to intensify its effect.

**6.8** Symptoms of opiate withdrawal are mediated by noradrenaline.

**6.9** Inconsistent parenting is associated with non-accidental injury.

**6.10** Confusion is a characteristic feature of night terrors.

**6.11** Learning disability is a risk factor for arson.

**6.12** Rett syndrome only occurs in females.

**6.13** Lilliputian hallucinations can be pleasant.

**6.14**    Pseudodementia generally has a more acute onset than dementia.

**6.15**    There is a strong association between substance misuse and acquisitive offending.

**6.16**    Shorter-acting benzodiazepines are more likely to induce dependence than longer-acting agents.

**6.17**    LSD (lysergic acid diethylamide) can cause a schizophreniform psychosis.

**6.18**    Excessive use of alcohol is a common cause of microcytic anaemia in outpatient populations.

**6.19**    Ventricular dilatation occurs in Wernicke's encephalopathy.

**6.20**    Low social class is a risk factor for excessive consumption of alcohol in the over-70s age range.

**6.21**    Excessive alcohol use is less common in Chinese than in Welsh populations.

**6.22**    Twelve-year-old boys have a prevalence of encopresis approximately four times that of girls of a similar age.

**6.23**    Boys are more likely to develop adjustment disorder in childhood than girls.

**6.24**    The gender incidence of late-onset schizophrenia is equal.

**6.25**    Empathy is reduced in autism but not in Asperger's syndrome.

**6.26**    Depressive disorders may present with food refusal in the elderly.

**6.27**    Countertransference refers to the specific emotional response aroused in the patient by the specific qualities of the analyst.

**6.28**    Transcortical motor aphasia is seen in Pick's disease.

**6.29** Phobic disorders are more prevalent than depression in people over 65 years of age.

**6.30** Down's syndrome accounts for more than 20% of all mental retardation.

**6.31** Down's syndrome is a risk factor for Alzheimer's disease and diabetes mellitus.

**6.32** Homozygosity for the e4 allele of apolipoprotein E on chromosome 19 is associated with late-onset Alzheimer's disease.

**6.33** The number of prisoners committing suicide has decreased over the last 15 years in the United Kingdom.

**6.34** Higher doses of antidepressants are needed in elderly patients as the response to a given dose is slower.

**6.35** Behaviourism involves environmentalism.

**6.36** Alzheimer's disease is characterised by relative preservation of memory in the presence of other areas of cognitive decline.

**6.37** Acute episodes of acute intermittent porphyria can be precipitated by nitrazepam and barbiturates.

**6.38** Munchausen syndrome is classified under factitious disorder in the 10th revision of the International Classification of Diseases (ICD-10).

**6.39** Transactional analysis deconstructs interpersonal interactions to examine the functions of communication.

**6.40** The relative risk of suicide in anorexia nervosa is 200.

**6.41** Family therapy is often practised with the help of input from professionals who observe the interview from behind a two-way mirror.

**6.42** Bright light therapy is better than dim light therapy in seasonal affective disorder.

**6.43** Cerebral lymphoma is a known complication of HIV infection.

**6.44** Schizophrenia is associated with tuberculosis.

**6.45** Acute akathisia is seen in almost a quarter of people receiving antipsychotics.

**6.46** Alpha rhythm is exaggerated in Huntington's disease.

**6.47** Schizophrenia is less common in people with learning difficulties than in the background population.

**6.48** Schizophrenia is associated with normal fertility.

**6.49** Ekbom syndrome may be a form of monosymptomatic hypochondriacal psychosis.

**6.50** Harmful use of alcohol is the most common co-morbid disorder with body dysmorphic disorder.

**6.51** Wilson's disease involves low serum copper and caeruloplasmin.

**6.52** Depression is especially common in Cushing's syndrome of pituitary origin.

**6.53** Heritability of bipolar disorder is higher than unipolar depressive disorder.

**6.54** A previous history of anorexia nervosa is common in bulimia nervosa.

**6.55** Mentally disordered offenders should be dealt with as far as possible in secure hospitals, away from potential victims.

**6.56** Ash leaf spots are characteristically seen in fragile X syndrome.

**6.57** Hydroxytryptophan is a useful treatment in Lesch–Nyhan syndrome.

**6.58** Fragile X syndrome characteristically involves tricuspid valve prolapse.

**6.59** Hyperorality is a recognised feature of frontotemporal dementia.

**6.60** Interpersonal therapy (ITP) is the most effective therapy in post-traumatic stress disorder.

**6.61** 40% of people committing suicide are dependent on alcohol.

**6.62** Alcohol dependence is associated with chromosome 4.

**6.63** Munchausen syndrome involves the deliberate production or simulation of symptoms for recognisable external motives.

**6.64** Behaviour therapy establishes links between behaviour and associated cognitions to provide a viable therapeutic intervention.

**6.65** Brain fag syndrome involves somatisation.

**6.66** Prejudice is effectively resolved by periods of physical separation between the two parties.

**6.67** Aspirin has potential for abuse.

**6.68** Unipolar depression breeds true.

**6.69** Onset of Huntington's disease in childhood is associated with cerebellar ataxia and epilepsy.

**6.70** Thirty per cent of people with Gilles de la Tourette's syndrome have an abnormal EEG.

**6.71** There is a strong association between depression and shoplifting in children.

**6.72**   Asthma in childhood predisposes to other conditions, including psychiatric disorder.

**6.73**   School refusal at the age of 5 years most commonly derives from separation anxiety.

**6.74**   Binswanger's disease is associated with pseudobulbar palsy.

**6.75**   Systematised delusions are seen more commonly in Lewy body than in vascular dementia.

**6.76**   Weight loss is a normal feature of bereavement.

**6.77**   Temporal lobe epilepsy in childhood is associated with a psychiatric disorder in most cases.

**6.78**   Redundant clothing is a feature of schizophrenia.

**6.79**   Children classically truant alone.

**6.80**   Appetite is characteristically reduced in anxiety.

**6.81**   Cocaine is associated with atherosclerosis and early myocardial infarction.

**6.82**   Splitting is a sophisticated defence mechanism.

**6.83**   Fire-setting can only be described as arson if it is committed as a result of mental illness.

**6.84**   Adopted children have a lifetime pattern of criminal behaviour closer to that of their adoptive than their biological parents.

**6.85**   Brachycephaly is associated with Down's syndrome.

**6.86**   Normalisation is discouraged within traditional therapeutic communities.

**6.87**   Parotid gland enlargement and pancreatitis are seen in anorexia nervosa.

**6.88** Digital paraesthesia is a feature of generalised anxiety disorder.

**6.89** Star charts are helpful in the management of enuresis.

**6.90** Naltrexone is a partial opioid agonist.

**6.91** Agitated depressive disorders are more common in the elderly than in young patients.

**6.92** The lifetime prevalence of phobic disorders is almost 10%.

**6.93** Mirtazepine increases rapid eye movement sleep.

**6.94** Those between the ages of 90 and 94 years are over 30 times more likely to suffer with dementia than those between the ages of 65 and 69 years.

**6.95** Autistic behaviour is seen in a wide range of conditions, including fragile X syndrome, rubella and tuberous sclerosis.

**6.96** Common law is made by Acts of Parliament.

**6.97** Orthodox behavioural therapy involves keeping diaries of thoughts and emotions.

**6.98** Trisomy X is associated with moderate learning disability.

**6.99** Transference can be used to investigate aspects of the self that are otherwise difficult to access.

**6.100** The mean age of onset of obsessive-compulsive disorder is lower in males.

**6.101** Long-term memory is affected early in Alzheimer's disease.

**6.102** Sleep-walking is most common between the ages of 5 and 8 years.

**6.103** Pseudobulbar palsy causes wasting of the tongue.

**6.104** An understanding of the relationship between an offender's mental state and their index offence is important in predicting future offending.

**6.105** Increased postnatal depression correlates with younger age at pregnancy, past psychiatric history and assisted delivery.

**6.106** There are approximately 60–70 homicides in the United Kingdom every year.

**6.107** Brushfield spots are suggestive of Down's syndrome.

**6.108** The distribution of prions is different in new variant Creutzfeldt–Jakob disease compared with Creutzfeldt–Jakob disease.

**6.109** Complications of anorexia include cardiac failure.

**6.110** Dysprosody is speech with loss of normal melody.

**6.111** A reduced thyroid-stimulating hormone response in depressive disorders correlates with treatment resistance.

**6.112** Near-death experiences occur in life-threatening situations.

**6.113** Paraphrenia more commonly affects men over 75 years of age than women over 75 years of age.

**6.114** Recurrent depressive disorder is a risk factor for dementia.

**6.115** The CAGE questionnaire involves asking patients if they feel guilt about their drinking.

**6.116** Cannabis improves reaction times.

**6.117** Elective mutism is more common in females than in males.

**6.118** Approximately 25% of children have been admitted to hospital by the age of 4 years.

**6.119** There is an association between childhood conduct disorder and affective disorder in later life.

**6.120** Most prisoners have social problems.

**6.121** Most prisoners in high-security prisons are psychotic.

**6.122** Down's syndrome is more common than fetal alcohol syndrome.

**6.123** There is an association between Klinefelter's syndrome and psychosis.

**6.124** Most children with autism have an IQ below 95.

**6.125** Dialectical behaviour therapy was originally conceived to help with social phobia.

**6.126** Cocaine and LSD (lysergic acid diethylamide) use are associated with formication.

**6.127** Patau's syndrome includes polycystic kidneys.

**6.128** Prion diseases are common.

**6.129** Computed tomography scans are sensitive and specific in diagnosis of Alzheimer's disease.

**6.130** Wernicke's encephalopathy characteristically develops over hours or even days.

**6.131** In hyperkinetic disorders, the motor restlessness characteristically increases during adolescence, as a result of the influence of increased testosterone production.

**6.132** Obsessive-compulsive disorder features depersonalisation as a characteristic feature.

**6.133** Cross-dressing typically starts before the age of 4 years in gender identity disorder.

**6.134** Distractible speech is more commonly a feature of schizophrenia than mania.

**6.135** Delusional perception is strongly suggestive of schizophrenia.

**6.136** The majority of perpetrators of homicide against children are parents or guardians.

**6.137** Most perpetrators of violence have difficulties with alcohol.

**6.138** Physical signs associated with anorexia nervosa include tetany, peripheral oedema and acute gastric dilation.

**6.139** Cannabis use can lead to an acute toxic psychosis.

**6.140** Children should be encouraged to discontinue temper tantrums by having a special treat every time a temper tantrum ceases.

**6.141** Coprophagia is an example of a vocal tic.

**6.142** Females are more at risk than males of developing Munchausen syndrome.

**6.143** Communicating hydrocephalus causes increased pressure on lumbar puncture.

**6.144** William's syndrome involves elfin facies and premature ageing of the skin.

**6.145** Huntington's disease has an age of onset which inversely correlates with the number of CCG repeats.

**6.146** Social phobia is the most common anxiety disorder in the elderly.

**6.147** Psychodynamic interpersonal therapy uses an exploratory approach mainly involving the use of questions.

**6.148** Psychiatric disorder is more common in prepubertal girls than boys.

**6.149** Orthopnoea suggests malingering.

**6.150** Risk factors for postpartum psychosis include low social class, young age at first child and having two or more children already.

**6.151** Unchanging affect is more suggestive of delirium than of dementia.

**6.152** Selective serotonin reuptake inhibitors (SSRIs) have been linked to an increased risk of suicide in adolescents with depressive disorders.

**6.153** Abnormal homicides include those committed as a result of personality disorder.

**6.154** A child who has a single parent affected by schizophrenia is less likely to be affected than a child with a single sibling with schizophrenia.

**6.155** Attachment behaviour is normal in children with autism.

**6.156** Attachment behaviour is disturbed in infantile autism.

**6.157** Exposure and response prevention may include the use of electric shocks.

**6.158** Fear of labour, neuroticism and a poor marital relationship predispose to postnatal blues.

**6.159** Normal syntactic structure is more likely in schizophrenia than of mania.

**6.160** Most trials of the efficacy of anti-dementia drugs demonstrate beneficial long-term effects which are sustained for at least 3 years.

**6.161** Delusional disorders presenting in the seventh decade of life are more common in women than in men.

**6.162** Wernicke's encephalopathy is caused by vitamin $B_2$ deficiency.

**6.163** The point prevalence of hyperkinetic disorder is 17%.

**6.164** Attachment behaviour is most marked between the ages of 2 and 4 years.

**6.165** Most homicides in the UK are committed by people with serious mental health problems.

# EXTENDED MATCHING ITEMS

### 6.166   THEME: TREATMENT OF ACUTE POISONING

| | |
|---|---|
| A | Acetylcysteine |
| B | Desferrioxamine |
| C | Dicobalt edetate |
| D | Dimercaprol |
| E | Flumazenil |
| F | Methionine |
| G | Naloxone |
| H | Oxygen |
| I | Penicillamine |
| J | Sodium nitrate |

**Choose the most appropriate intervention from the list above for each of the following situations:**

1   A 24-year-old woman presents to Accident and Emergency having taken 12g of paracetamol 4 hours ago. Her plasma paracetamol concentration is above the normal treatment line.

2   A 29-year-old inpatient on a general psychiatric ward is found in the bathroom with respiratory compromise and pinpoint pupils.

3   A 67-year-old man is brought to the hospital having been found in his old car, with the engine running and a hosepipe connecting the exhaust to the interior.

## 6.167    THEME: DRUG INTERACTIONS

| | |
|---|---|
| A | Increased plasma concentration of antipsychotic |
| B | Increased plasma concentration of benzodiazepine |
| C | Increased risk of agranulocytosis |
| D | Increased risk of neurotoxicity |
| E | Increased sedative effect |
| F | Neuroprotective effect |
| G | Reduced anticoagulant effect of coumarins |
| H | Reduced plasma concentration of antipsychotic |
| I | Reduced plasma concentration of benzodiazepine |
| J | Renal impairment |

Choose the most likely interaction from the list above for each of the following:

1    Alcohol and antipsychotics.
2    Carbamazepine and risperidone.
3    Fluoxetine and clozapine.
4    Fluvoxamine and a benzodiazepine.
5    Lithium and a selective serotonin reuptake inhibitor (SSRI).

## 6.168   THEME: CLASSIFICATION OF MENTAL DISORDERS

| | |
|---|---|
| A | F00–09 – Organic including symptomatic mental disorders |
| B | F10–19 |
| C | F20–29 – Schizophrenia, schizotypal and delusional disorders |
| D | F30–39 – Affective disorders |
| E | F40–48 – Neurotic, stress-related and somatoform disorders |
| F | F50–59 – Behavioural syndromes related to physiological disturbance and physical factors |
| G | F60–69 |
| H | F70–79 |
| I | F80–89 |
| J | F90–98 – Behavioural and emerging diseases of childhood and adolescence |

**Choose the section of the 10th revision of the International Classification of Diseases (ICD-10) from the list above which is used to classify each of the following:**

| | |
|---|---|
| 1 | Delirium tremens |
| 2 | Post-schizophrenic depression |
| 3 | Multiple personality disorder |
| 4 | Eating disorders. |

### 6.169   THEME: CATATONIA

| | |
|---|---|
| A | Advertence |
| B | Ambitendence |
| C | Automatic obedience |
| D | Echopraxia |
| E | Mannerism |
| F | Mitmachen |
| G | Obstruction |
| H | Opposition |
| I | Stereotypy |
| J | Waxy flexibility |

**Choose the term from the list above which relates to each of the following behaviours:**

1   A posture is maintained for long periods. If the posture is altered by another person moving parts of the body, the new posture is maintained in the same way.

2   Any attempt by another person to alter the posture is met with just enough pressure to resist the alteration in posture, without moving.

3   Movements are carried out which are meaningless and not goal-directed.

4   Posture is altered in response to light pressure. When the pressure is released, the previous posture is resumed.

5   A goal-directed movement is performed in an unusual and atypical manner.

## 6.170   THEME: HALLUCINATORY EXPERIENCES

| | |
|---|---|
| A | Ecmnesic hallucinations |
| B | Extracampine hallucinations |
| C | Hallucinosis |
| D | Haptic hallucinations |
| E | Hypnagogic hallucinations |
| F | Imperative hallucinations |
| G | Kinaesthetic hallucinations |
| H | Lilliputian hallucinations |
| I | Reflex hallucinations |
| J | Typical schizophrenic hallucinations |

**Choose the term from the above list which most accurately describes each of the following:**

1   Second or third person auditory hallucinations which are inconsistently literalised and increased with reduced sensory input and drowsiness.

2   Hallucinations occurring outside the sensorium.

3   Hallucinations occurring in one modality in response to a stimulus in another.

4   Hallucinations occurring only in the presence of an unrelated stimulus in the same modality.

5   Auditory hallucinations characteristically involving hearing one's name spoken aloud.

## 6.171    THEME: EEG PHENOMENA

A          Decreased alpha rhythms
B          Decreased delta rhythms
C          Decreased spikes
D          Flat trace
E          Increased alpha rhythms
F          Increased beta rhythms
G          Increased delta rhythms
H          Increased lambda rhythms
I          Increased waves
J          Reduced theta rhythms

**Choose the most likely effect on the EEG from the list above for each of the following:**

1          Delirium tremens.
2          Hepatic encephalopathy.
3          Opening of the eyes.

# PRACTICE PAPER 6

## Answers

### INDIVIDUAL STATEMENT QUESTIONS

**6.1** **False** – They are seen in Rett's syndrome.

**6.2** **True**
A–Z p260–3

**6.3** **True** – This is an inability to make decisions.

**6.4** **True** – It involves difficulty in word finding.
A–Z p41

**6.5** **True**
A–Z p209

**6.6** **False** – They are usually brightly coloured.
A–Z p62

**6.7** **False** – It is smoked or taken orally.

**6.8** **True**
Fear p487

**6.9** **True**

**6.10** **True**
A–Z p225

**6.11** **False** – This was once thought to be the case.

**6.12** **False** – This was originally believed to be the case, but it does occur in males.

**6.13** **True** – They involve little people or small animals.

**6.14** **True**

**6.15** **True**

**6.16** **True**

**6.17** **True**

**6.18** **False** – It is a common cause of macrocytic anaemia.

**6.19** **True**
A–Z p343–5

**6.20** **False** – Low social class is protective. High social class is a risk factor.

**6.21** **True** – As a result of the common variant of alcohol dehydrogenase in Chinese populations.

**6.22** **True** – It is 1.3% in boys and 0.3% in girls.

**6.23** **True**

**6.24** **False** – It is much more common in females.

**6.25** **False** – It is reduced in both.

**6.26** **True**
A–Z p11

**6.27** **False** – Countertransference relates to the emotional response of the analyst to the patient.
A–Z p87

**6.28** **True** – This is similar to Broca's aphasia, but the ability to repeat sentences is well preserved.
A–Z p41, 256

**6.29** **False** – Depression is slightly more common.

**6.30** **True** – It accounts for approximately 30%.

**6.31** **True**

**6.32** **True**
A–Z p106–10, Fear p449

**6.33** **False** – It has risen dramatically.

**6.34** **False** – The response may be slower but lower doses may be appropriate as plasma levels are generally higher than in younger patients.
Fear p464

**6.35** **True** – Environmentalism is the belief that all organisms are shaped by the environment and learn from experience.
A–Z p58

**6.36** **False** – There is early deterioration of memory.

**6.37** **True**
A–Z p258–9

**6.38** **False** – It is classified under factitious disorder in the Diagnostic and Statistical Manual of Mental Disorders (DSM-IV) and as a personality disorder in 10th revision of the International Classification of Diseases (ICD-10).
A–Z p218–19

**6.39** **True**

**6.40** **True**
A–Z p26–9

**6.41** **True**

**6.42** **False** – No difference has been demonstrated.

**6.43** **True**

**6.44** **True**
A–Z p281–6

**6.45** **True**
A–Z p19

**6.46** **False** – It is practically abolished.
A–Z p167–9

**6.47** **False** – It is significantly more common.

**6.48** **False** – It is associated with low fertility.
A–Z p281–6

**6.49** **True**

**6.50** **False** – Personality disorder and psychosis are the most common co-morbid disorders.

**6.51** **True** – With increased urinary copper.
A–Z p112–13

**6.52** **True**

**6.53** **True**
A–Z p8–14

**6.54** **True**
A–Z p26–9

**6.55** **False** – They should be dealt with in the community, as far as this is possible.

**6.56** **False** – They are seen in tuberous sclerosis.

**6.57** **True** – It can reduce self-mutilation.
A–Z p194–5

**6.58** **False** – Mitral valve prolapse is seen in 75%.

**6.58** **False** – Mitral valve prolapse is seen in 75%.

**6.59** **True** – It is characteristic.
Fear p453

**6.60**  **False** – Cognitive behavioural therapy is more appropriate in most cases.

**6.61**  **False** – 20%.
A–Z p310–11

**6.62**  **True** – There is a region of chromosome 4 which is protective against alcohol dependence.

**6.63**  Munchausen's syndrome involves the deliberate production or simulation of symptoms for recognisable external motives.

**6.63**  **False** – This describes malingering. The motives in Munchausen syndrome are more obscure.
A–Z p44

**6.64**  **False** – Behaviour therapy disregards cognitions and focuses on behaviour.
A–Z p320

**6.65**  **True**

**6.66**  **False** – Physical separation increases prejudice.

**6.67**  **True** – Almost all prescribed and over-the-counter medications have some potential for abuse.

**6.68**  **True** – This means that relatives of people with unipolar depression are more likely to experience unipolar depression but not bipolar disorder, compared with the general population.

**6.69**  **True**
A–Z p167–9

**6.70**  **True**

**6.71**  **False**

**6.72**  **True**

**6.73** **True**

**6.74** **True**

**6.75** **True**

**6.76** **True**

**6.77** **False** – Only in one-third of cases.
A–Z p137

**6.78** **True**

**6.79** **False** – They usually truant in groups.

**6.80** **True**
A–Z p38–9

**6.81** **True**

**6.82** **False** – It is very primitive.

**6.83** **False**

**6.84** **False** – It is more like their biological parents' pattern.

**6.85** **True**

**6.86** **False** – It is one of the main aims of therapeutic communities and involves restoring deviant behaviour to more closely resemble social norms.

**6.87** **True**
A–Z p26–9

**6.88** **True**
A–Z p114–15

**6.89** **True** – Although approximately 50% relapse.
A–Z p135

**6.90**    **False** – It is an opioid antagonist.

**6.91**    **True**

**6.92**    **True**

**6.93**    **False** – It reduces rapid eye movement sleep.

**6.94**    **True**
Fear p445

**6.95**    **True**

**6.96**    **False** – It is made by judges setting precedents. Acts of Parliament make 'statute law'.

**6.97**    **False** – It concentrates solely on behaviour.

**6.98**    **False** – IQ is in the normal, borderline or mild learning disability range.

**6.99**    **True**

**6.100**    **True** – It is 20 years in females.
A–Z p230–1

**6.101**    **False**

**6.102**    **False** – Between the ages of 7 and 13 years.

**6.103**    **False** – Bulbar palsy causes tongue wasting.
A–Z p236

**6.104**    **True**

**6.105**    **False** – There is no relationship with assisted delivery.
A–Z p259–60

**6.106**    **False** – There are 700.

**6.107**    **True** – They are also seen in normal children but are more

common in Down's syndrome. They are white spots on the
iris in a ring around the pupil.

**6.108** **True** – New variant Creutzfeldt–Jakob disease involves higher
concentrations in the brainstem, cerebellum and cortex.
A–Z p110–11

**6.109** **True**
A–Z p26–9

**6.110** **True**

**6.111** **False**

**6.112** **True**

**6.113** **False** – It is more common in females.
A–Z p239

**6.114** **True** – Alzheimer's disease.

**6.115** **True** – CAGE is a series of four questions about **C**ontrol of
drinking, whether people are **A**nnoyed about your drinking,
whether you feel **G**uilty about your drinking and whether you
ever have an **E**ye-opener (an early morning drink).

**6.116** **False** – It impairs reaction times.

**6.117** **False** – The sex incidence is equal.

**6.118** **True**

**6.119** **True**

**6.120** **True**

**6.121** **False**

**6.122** **False** – Fetal alcohol syndrome is (just) more common.

**6.123** **True** – There appears to be a weak association.

**6.124**   **True**

**6.125**   **False** – Borderline personality disorder.

**6.126**   **False** – This is true only for cocaine.

**6.127**   **True**

**6.128**   **False** – They are rare.
Fear p455

**6.129**   **False**

**6.130**   **False** – It has an acute onset.

**6.131**   **False** – It decreases during adolescence.

**6.132**   **True** – It also features anxiety and depression.

**6.133**   **True**

**6.134**   **False** – It is more common in mania.

**6.135**   **True** – It is a first-rank symptom.

**6.136**   **True** – Over 75%.

**6.137**   **True** – It is just over 50%.

**6.138**   **True**
A–Z p26–9

**6.139**   **True**

**6.140**   **False** – They should not receive any special attention.

**6.141**   **False** – This refers to ingestion of faeces. Coprophilia (use of obscene language) is a vocal tic.

**6.142**   **False** – It is more common in men.

**6.143**   **True**
A–Z p169

**6.144**   **True**

**6.145**   **False** – This is all true, but the repeats are CAG, not CCG.
A–Z p167–9

**6.146**   **False** – Simple phobia and agoraphobia are more common.
Fear p459

**6.147**   **False** – The aim is to share feelings and reach a shared
understanding. Questioning is not a prominent feature of this
process.
A–Z p321

**6.148**   **False** – The male : female ratio is 2 : 1.

**6.149**   **False** – It is highly suggestive of cardiac failure.

**6.150**   **False** – Risk factors are high social class, older age at first
child and having no children.

**6.151**   **False** – It suggests dementia.

**6.152**   **True**

**6.153**   **True**

**6.154**   **True** – Uniparental schizophrenia confers a lifetime risk of 6%,
a sibling with schizophrenia confers a lifetime risk of 10%.
A–Z p287–91

**6.155**   **False**
A–Z p53

**6.156**   **True**
A–Z p53

**6.157**   **False** – Not in any clinically useful setting.

**6.156** **True**
A–Z p53

**6.157** **False** – Not in any clinically useful setting.

**6.158** **True**
A–Z p259

**6.159** **False** – The reverse is true.
A–Z p202

**6.160** **False** – Most trials do not support evidence for benefit lasting more than 2 years.

**6.161** **True**

**6.162** **False** – Vitamin $B_1$.

**6.163** **False** – About 2%.

**6.164** **False** – Between the ages of 6 months and 3 years.
A–Z p46–7

**6.165** **False** – It is less than 30%.

## EXTENDED MATCHING ITEMS

### 6.166 THEME: TREATMENT OF ACUTE POISONING

1    **A** – Acetylcysteine
2    **G** – Naloxone
3    **H** – Oxygen

### 6.167 THEME: DRUG INTERACTIONS

1    **E** – Increased sedative effect
2    **H** – Reduced plasma concentration of antipsychotic because
     of enzyme induction by carbamazepine
3    **A** – Increased plasma concentration of antipsychotic
4    **B** – Increased plasma concentration of benzodiazepine
5    **D** – Increased risk of neurotxicity

### 6.168 THEME: CLASSIFICATION OF MENTAL DISORDERS

1    **B** – F10–19 (Disorders relating to use of dependence-
     producing substances)
2    **C** – F20–29 – Schizophrenia, schizotypal and delusional
     disorders
3    **E** – F40–48 – Neurotic, stress-related and somatoform
     disorders
4    **F** – F50–59 – Behavioural syndromes related to physiological
     disturbance and physical factors

### 6.169 THEME: CATATONIA

1    **J** – Waxy flexibility
2    **H** – Opposition
3    **I** – Stereotypy
4    **F** – Mitmachen
5    **E** – Mannerism

## 6.170   THEME: HALLUCINATORY EXPERIENCES

| | |
|---|---|
| I | **J** – Typical schizophrenic hallucinations |
| 2 | **B** – Extracampine hallucinations |
| 3 | **I** – Reflex hallucinations |
| 4 | **C** – Hallucinosis |
| 5 | **E** – Hypnagogic hallucinations |
| | A–Z p159–62 |

## 6.171   THEME: EEG PHENOMENA

| | |
|---|---|
| I | **F** – Increased beta rhythms |
| 2 | **G** – Increased delta rhythms |
| 3 | **H** – Increased lambda rhythms |
| | A–Z p365–6 |

# PRACTICE PAPER 7

*Time allowed: 90 minutes*

## INDIVIDUAL STATEMENT QUESTIONS

**7.1**    Self-mutilation is common in anorexia nervosa.

**7.2**    Mild memory disturbance is an absolute contraindication to cognitive behaviour therapy in the elderly.

**7.3**    Increasing taxes on alcohol leads to reduced consumption.

**7.4**    Acamprosate can help patients achieve abstinence from alcohol use.

**7.5**    Loperamide has a role in management of opiate withdrawal.

**7.6**    Encopresis has an equal sex incidence.

**7.7**    According to the 10th revision of the International Classification of Diseases (ICD-10), mild mental retardation involves an IQ of 60–69.

**7.8**    Offences committed by people with schizophrenia are characteristically violent and usually very serious.

**7.9**    Cognitive behavioural therapy is often helpful in bulimia nervosa.

**7.10**   Lesch–Nyhan syndrome affects males and females equally.

**7.11**   Multinucleated giant cells derived from tanycytes are seen in cerebral HIV infection.

**7.12**   Miller–Dieker syndrome results in profound learning difficulty.

**7.13** Epilepsy in children is associated with severe mental retardation more commonly than with mild mental retardation.

**7.14** Obsessive-compulsive disorder (OCD) in childhood has a poor prognosis, with two-thirds of children developing other long-term problems.

**7.15** An association has been suggested between hypocholesterolaemia and tendency to suicide.

**7.16** Mentally disordered offenders should be treated quite a long way from their previous community to minimise disruptive and negative influences.

**7.17** The HCR-20 assesses depressive symptoms so that suicide can be predicted.

**7.18** Of people committing homicide, a higher proportion of females are unwell than males.

**7.19** In males, the XYY and XYYY patterns cause a marked increase in interpersonal violence and pro-criminal behaviour, without an associated increase in dissocial personality disorder.

**7.20** Direct, closed questions should be used throughout an interview with an adolescent, to guide them appropriately.

**7.21** In paedophilia, the risk of future offending correlates with the extent of previous offending.

**7.22** There is a strong association between Edward's syndrome and learning difficulties.

**7.23** Psychodynamic interpersonal therapy involves focusing on negative cognitions.

**7.24** Thirty-five per cent of children have a chronic illness.

**7.25** Couvade syndrome is very rare.

**7.26** Gilles de la Tourette syndrome is more common in males.

**7.27** Temporal lobe epilepsy can be confused with an anxiety state.

**7.28** Clumsiness is associated with hyperkinetic disorders in childhood.

**7.29** The bell and pad method of management of enuresis is generally ineffective.

**7.30** Postpartum psychosis is characterised by cognitive impairment.

**7.31** Communicating hydrocephalus causes increased pressure on lumbar puncture.

**7.32** There is a significant association between hyperkinetic disorders and peer-group rejection in 9-year-old boys.

**7.33** The highest risk group for suicide in the United Kingdom is men over 75 years of age.

**7.34** Attachment behaviour is characterised by seeking proximity, separation distress and the secure base effect.

**7.35** The severity of anxiety in depressive disorders usually correlates with the severity of the depressive symptoms.

**7.36** School refusal at the age of 15 years may result from a depressive disorder.

**7.37** Moderate alcohol consumption may have a protective effect against Alzheimer's disease.

**7.38** Panic attacks can cause chest pain and rotational nystagmus.

**7.39** Dhat involves coprolalia, echolalia and echopraxia.

**7.40** Pick's disease has an equal sex distribution.

**7.41** The Edinburgh Postnatal Depression Scale was designed to assess the severity of postnatal depressive disorders.

**7.42** Hallucinogens can cause flashbacks which may occur years after exposure to the hallucinogen.

**7.43** Depressive disorders are more common in people who are married.

**7.44** Kleine–Levine syndrome features hypersexuality.

**7.45** Selective serotonin reuptake inhibitors (SSRIs) are recommended for use in Alzheimer's disease with co-morbid depressive features because there are relatively few anticholinergic effects.

**7.46** The prevalence of depressive disorders in the elderly is 25%.

**7.47** Periodic limb movement disorder is a recognised condition occurring in 5% of people over 60 years.

**7.48** Automatism is a common feature in catatonia.

**7.49** TWEAK is an appropriate screening test for alcoholism in males with challenging behaviour.

**7.50** Depressive pseudodementia is synonymous with dissociative pseudodementia.

**7.51** Cotard's syndrome is most common in single elderly males.

**7.52** Patients with a diagnosis of dementia should not be told of their diagnosis as they are likely to forget it and will be distressed.

**7.53** Near-death experiences involve depersonalisation.

**7.54** Delusions and hallucinations are features of most cases of paraphrenia.

**7.55** Unipolar depression has a poorer prognosis in females.

**7.56** Approximately one-quarter of people with anorexia nervosa binge eat.

**7.57** Post-traumatic stress disorder is particularly common in firefighters.

**7.58** Fifty per cent of new mothers experience postnatal blues.

**7.59** There is a strong association between ADHD and conduct disorder.

**7.60** Pregnancy is protective against suicide.

**7.61** Punning and clanging are most commonly encountered in manic states.

**7.62** Mental illness inevitably causes unfitness to plead.

**7.63** Benzodiazepine withdrawal can cause derealisation.

**7.64** Somatic symptoms of severe anxiety include impotence, hyperventilation and diarrhoea.

**7.65** The CAGE questionnaire involves asking patients about violence associated with their drinking.

**7.66** Denial is a defence mechanism which is prominent amongst users of cocaine.

**7.67** Cannabis use has a strong association with acquisitive offending.

**7.68** Central pontine myelinosis causes psychosis.

**7.69** A poor prognosis in depressive disorders in the elderly is indicated by ventricular dilatation on computed tomography and white matter changes on magnetic resonance imaging.

**7.70** Hirschsprung's disease is often a feature of Down's syndrome.

**7.71** Countertransference is an obstacle to treatment.

**7.72** Cognitive analytic therapy is usually long term.

**7.73** Autism is usually a feature of tuberous sclerosis.

**7.74** Four-year-olds are commonly fussy eaters.

**7.75** Elective mutism is associated with a sensitive personality.

**7.76** Brain biopsy is clinically useful in diagnosis of Alzheimer's disease.

**7.77** Speech disorders in Alzheimer's disease include poverty of content of speech and repeated asking of questions.

**7.78** The prevalence of dementia rises exponentially with age.

**7.79** Hurler syndrome presents in the first or second year of life with macrocephaly and coarse facies. The long-term prognosis is good.

**7.80** Rapid fluctuations are more characteristic of delirium than of dementia.

**7.81** Behavioural disorders are associated with learning disability in tuberous sclerosis.

**7.82** Risk factors for obsessive-compulsive disorder include IQ above 100 and high social class.

**7.83** The risk of suicide in schizophrenia is increased by akathisia, unemployment and high educational achievement.

**7.84** Schizophrenia more commonly affects people born in autumn and winter, possibly as a result of viral infections causing stress on developing neural tissue.

**7.85** Tetrabenazine frequently exacerbates the movement disorder in Huntington's disease.

**7.86** Hypochondriasis may co-exist with a physical disorder.

**7.87** Lewy body dementia is associated with repeated falls and sensitivity to antipsychotic medication.

**7.88** Heterozygosity of the e4 allele of apolipoprotein E is a risk factor for late-onset Alzheimer's disease.

**7.89** There is a positive correlation between IQ and social class.

**7.90** Most children killed under the age of 1 year are killed by their mother.

**7.91** Risk factors for psychiatric disorder in childhood include maternal depressive disorders and a poor relationship between the parents.

**7.92** As Korsakoff's syndrome progresses, the associated confabulation becomes momentary rather than fantastic.

**7.93** Visual hallucinations can result from solvent abuse, procyclidine abuse and cannabis abuse.

**7.94** Asperger's syndrome is similar to autism, but is characterised by normal intellectual development and language development in many cases.

**7.95** Above average height is interpreted as increased confidence by others.

**7.96** Irritable bowel syndrome may be relieved in part by brief psychodynamic psychotherapy.

**7.97** Orthogonal symptoms of schizophrenia are neither positive nor negative.

**7.98** Emotional lability is seen in Wernicke's encephalopathy.

**7.99** Kayser–Fleischer rings are seen over the sclera in Wilson's disease.

**7.100** Diogenes' syndrome is associated with frontal lobe dysfunction.

**7.101** The heritability of conduct disorder is 0.1–0.2.

**7.102** Ash leaf spots suggest a diagnosis of tuberous sclerosis.

**7.103** Ecstasy acts as a hallucinogen but not a stimulant.

**7.104** Anorexia nervosa can involve self-induced vomiting and purging.

**7.105** Depression in the elderly is associated with cognitive impairment in 10–20%.

**7.106** Prominent affective symptoms are associated with a good prognosis in schizophrenia.

**7.107** Postnatal blues are characterised by tearfulness, emotional lability and confusion.

**7.108** Phobic anxiety is subjectively different from other forms of anxiety.

**7.109** Cycloid psychoses typically have a good outcome.

**7.110** Diogenes' syndrome is more common in females.

**7.111** The ataxia in Wernicke's encephalopathy is mild or moderate, but never severe.

**7.112** Physical dependence can result from LSD (lysergic acid diethylamide) but not MDMA use.

**7.113** First-degree relatives of people with Tourette's syndrome have a significantly increased prevalence of tic disorder.

**7.114** Male children show more distress than female children when mothers remarry.

**7.115** Conviction rates may be influenced by the fact that offenders with learning disability are more likely to be caught.

**7.116** Violent offenders have a characteristic EEG trace.

**7.117**  Fragile X syndrome is associated with coarse skin.

**7.118**  The ideas of transference and countertransference are only applicable within the psychotherapeutic relationship.

**7.119**  Projection is a primitive defence mechanism.

**7.120**  A diagnosis of schizophrenia within a key family member is a relative contraindication to family therapy.

**7.121**  According to Vaughn and Leff, relapses in unipolar depression are increased in the presence of a highly critical spouse.

**7.122**  Osteoporosis is a late complication of anorexia nervosa.

**7.123**  Subacute sclerosing panencephalitis causes increased pressure on lumbar puncture.

**7.124**  Therapists in cognitive behavioural therapy are guided by the patient, who takes the initiative with regard to the content of the session.

**7.125**  The 10th version of the International Classification of Diseases (ICD-10) criteria for schizophrenia are more restrictive than the criteria in the fourth revision of the Diagnostic and Statistical Manual of Mental Disorders (DSM-IV).

**7.126**  Over 75% of users of opiates have a criminal history.

**7.127**  Postpartum psychosis features prominent affective symptoms and is characterised by depressive symptoms.

**7.128**  Night terrors occur in the last third of the night and are genetically linked to sleep-walking.

**7.129**  Dietary exclusion may be useful in the investigation of hyperkinetic disorders of childhood.

**7.130**  Homicide accounts for most violent deaths in the United Kingdom.

**7.131** Fulminant hepatic necrosis is the most frequent cause of death in adults with Down's syndrome.

**7.132** Depression is common in obsessive-compulsive disorder.

**7.133** Depressive pseudodementia is a risk factor for dementia.

**7.134** Khat use can precipitate an abnormal mood state resembling a manic episode.

**7.135** Increased α-activity on the EEG is associated with an increased risk of alcohol dependence.

**7.136** Difficulty turning is characteristic of normal pressure hydrocephalus.

**7.137** Munchausen's syndrome correlates strongly with alcohol and opiate dependence.

**7.138** Extrapyramidal features are a feature of Alzheimer's disease.

**7.139** One-third of victims of rape did not know their attacker previously.

**7.140** The attendance of the patient at sessions is the best indicator of outcome.

**7.141** Difficulties in reading are more common in China than in the United Kingdom.

**7.142** Cocaine blocks dopamine reuptake.

**7.143** Buprenorphine is an opioid antagonist.

**7.144** Anticholinergics are an effective treatment for akathisia.

**7.145** Ataxia is a feature of Ganser's syndrome.

**7.146** Sleep-walking occurs during stage 2 of sleep.

**7.147** Acute intermittent porphyria usually involves seizures.

**7.148**    Anti-mentalism is a feature of psychoanalytic theory.

**7.149**    Late-onset schizophrenia has a better prognosis than early onset schizophrenia.

**7.150**    Rivastigmine may be of benefit in Lewy body dementia.

**7.151**    There is an association between child sexual abuse and weakened sexual identity in the victim.

**7.152**    Turner's syndrome characteristically leads to mild learning difficulties.

**7.153**    Huntington's disease typically presents in middle age.

**7.154**    The presence of circumstantiality suggests a diagnosis of mania rather than schizophrenia.

**7.155**    Cathartic colon is associated with anorexia nervosa.

**7.156**    Generalised anxiety disorder has a prevalence of about 14%.

**7.157**    Herpes simplex encephalitis causes frontal lobe symptoms.

**7.158**    Bonnet's syndrome involves hallucinations which are only ever fleeting and elementary.

**7.159**    Cannabis use can lead to gynaecomastia.

**7.160**    There is an association between encopresis and nocturnal enuresis.

**7.161**    Bottom shuffling is associated with a delay in walking.

**7.162**    Most perpetrators of indecent exposure go on to sexually assault their victims.

**7.163**    A single transverse palmar crease is pathognomonic of intellectual impairment.

**7.164** Degree of learning difficulty is recorded on Axis IV of the fourth revision of the Diagnostic and Statistical Manual of Mental Disorders (DSM-IV).

**7.165** Dialectical behaviour therapy is usually practiced on an individual basis and not in groups.

# EXTENDED MATCHING ITEMS

## 7.166 THEME: TREATMENT IN DRUG ADDICTION

| | |
|---|---|
| A | Acamprosate |
| B | Buprenorphine |
| C | Buproprion |
| D | Cocodamol |
| E | Diamorphine |
| F | Lofexidine |
| G | Methadone |
| H | Naloxone |
| I | Naltrexone |
| J | Paracetamol |

**Choose the most appropriate substance from the list above for each of the following:**

1    A patient with a history of alcohol dependence is currently abstinent and wishes to remain so.

2    A patient with a history of opiate dependence is now free from medication and wants help to prevent relapse.

3    A patient currently using heroin on a daily basis wants help to stop.

## 7.167 THEME: CLINICAL SYNDROMES

| | |
|---|---|
| A | Asperger's syndrome |
| B | Capgras's syndrome |
| C | Cotard's syndrome |
| D | De Clerambault's syndrome |
| E | Down's syndrome |
| F | Ganser's syndrome |
| G | Klinefelter's syndrome |
| H | Munchausen's syndrome |
| I | Tourette's syndrome |
| J | Turner's syndrome |

**Identify the most appropriate descriptive term from the list above for each of the following:**

1    A 45-year-old woman who believes that her husband has been replaced by an imposter who is physically identical to him.
2    A 78-year-old woman who believes herself, her family and her house have never existed.
3    A single woman who believes that a pop star is in love with her and intends to meet her shortly to declare undying love.
4    A short person with a thick neck and normal intelligence.

## 7.168  THEME: DIAGNOSIS

| | |
|---|---|
| A | Alzheimer's disease |
| B | Couvade's syndrome |
| C | Diogenes' syndrome |
| D | Friedriech's ataxia |
| E | Ganser's syndrome |
| F | Gerstmann's syndrome |
| G | Kluver–Bucy syndrome |
| H | Medial medullary syndrome |
| I | Post-traumatic stress disorder |
| J | Temporal lobe epilepsy |

**Choose the condition from the list above most closely associated with each of the following:**

| | |
|---|---|
| 1 | Hypertrophic obstructive cardiomyopathy |
| 2 | Dysphasia |
| 3 | Forced thinking |
| 4 | Finger agnosia |
| 5 | Approximate answers |

### 7.169    THEME: MOVEMENT DISORDER

| | |
|---|---|
| A | Ambitendence |
| B | Choreiform movements |
| C | Cogwheel rigidity |
| D | Epileptiform seizures |
| E | Facial twitching |
| F | Myoclonic jerks |
| G | Salaam attacks |
| H | Tics |
| I | Waxy flexibility |
| J | Wide-based, lurching gait |

**Choose the abnormal movement from the list above most closely associated with each of the following disorders:**

1    Parkinson's disease
2    Wilson's disease
3    Creutzfeld–Jakob disease
4    Tourette's syndrome.

## 7.170 THEME: PREVENTION

| | |
|---|---|
| A | Early intervention services for first-episode psychosis |
| B | Educating primary school children about the dangers of smoking |
| C | Providing staffed hostel accommodation for recently discharged people with schizophrenia |
| D | Supportive psychotherapy to improve compliance with antipsychotics |
| E | The Changing Minds Campaign led by the Royal College of Psychiatrists |
| F | The Partners in Care Programme |

**Choose two interventions from the list above which are described by each of the following:**

| | |
|---|---|
| 1 | Primary prevention. |
| 2 | Secondary prevention. |
| 3 | Tertiary prevention. |

## 7.171  THEME: CULTURE-BOUND SYNDROMES

| | |
|---|---|
| A | Amok |
| B | Brain fag syndrome |
| C | Dhat |
| D | Grisi siknis |
| E | Hwa-byong |
| F | Koro |
| G | Latah |
| H | Mal de ojo |
| I | Piblokto |
| J | Windigo |

**Choose the correct term from the list above for each of the following:**

1    A fear that the penis will withdraw into the abdomen, causing death. This can cause the sufferer to attach string or clamps to the penis to prevent its retraction.

2    Weakness, malaise, lethargy and poor concentration, associated with shame about masturbation. The sufferer attributes the symptoms to a loss of semen.

3    Exaggerated startle response accompanied by echopraxia, echolalia, automatic obedience, coprolalia and suggestibility.

**Identify the condition from the list above affecting the following groups:**

4    Young Inuit women

5    Native Americans

6    Young West Africans.

## 7.172  THEME: PROGNOSIS IN SCHIZOPHRENIA

| | |
|---|---|
| A | Female gender |
| B | Higher social class |
| C | Insidious onset |
| D | Keeping pets |
| E | Lower social class |
| F | Male gender |
| G | Older age at first onset |
| H | Rapid onset |
| I | Smoking more than 20 cigarettes dail |
| J | Younger age at first onset |

**Identify two items from the above list for each of the following:**

1  Factors relating to the onset of schizophrenia indicating a good prognosis.
2  Sociodemographic factors indicating a poor prognosis in schizophrenia.
3  Factors which have no predictive value.

# PRACTICE PAPER 7

## Answers

### INDIVIDUAL STATEMENT QUESTIONS

**7.1**    **True** – It occurs in over 50%.
A–Z p26–9

**7.2**    **False** – It is a relative contraindication.

**7.3**    **True**
Fear p477

**7.4**    **False** – It is helpful in maintaining abstinence, after it has been achieved.

**7.5**    **True** – Its role is in managing diarrhoea.
Fear p488

**7.6**    **False** – It is much more common in boys (4 : 1).

**7.7**    **False** – It involves an IQ of 50–59.

**7.8**    **False** – They are most often non-violent.

**7.9**    **True**
Fear p512

**7.10**    **False** – It is an X-linked recessive disorder.

**7.11**    **False** – They are derived from macrocytes.

**7.12**    **True**

**7.13**    **True**

**7.14**    **False** – The prognosis is good and only one-third have long-term problems.

**7.15**   **True**
A–Z p310–11

**7.16**   **False** – They should be treated as near as practicable to their friends and family.

**7.17**   **False** – It is an assessment of risk of future violence. HCR stands for **H**istorical, **C**linical and **R**isk management.

**7.18**   **True** – Most female perpetrators of homicide are unwell.

**7.19**   **False**

**7.20**   **False** – This may seem threatening.

**7.21**   **True** – This is the case for many types of crime.

**7.22**   **True**

**7.23**   **False**
A–Z p321

**7.24**   **False** – 15%.

**7.25**   **False** – It is rare, but not very rare.

**7.26**   **False** – It is three to four times more common in females.

**7.27**   **True**
A–Z p137

**7.28**   **True**

**7.29**   **False** – It is a useful method and is regarded as the most effective.
A–Z p135

**7.30**   **False**

**7.31**   **True**
A–Z p169

**7.32**    **True**

**7.33**    **True**

**7.34**    **True**
       A–Z p46–7

**7.35**    **False**
       A–Z p38–9

**7.36**    **True**

**7.37**    **True**
       Fear p449

**7.38**    **False** – Not rotational nystagmus.

**7.39**    **False** – These are seen in latah.
       A–Z p362–3

**7.40**    **False** – It is more common in women than men.
       A–Z p256

**7.41**    **False** – It is a screening tool.

**7.42**    True

**7.43**    **False**

**7.44**    **True**
       A–Z p187

**7.45**    **True**
       Fear p464

**7.46**    **False** – It is 5%.
       Fear p456

**7.47**    **False** – It occurs in 35% of over-60-year-olds.
       A–Z p115

PAPER 7
ANSWERS

**7.48**    **False** – It is seen in epilepsy.

**7.49**    **False** – It is for use in pregnant women. The questions relate to Tolerance, Worry about drink, Eye-openers, Amnesia, and Cutting down.
Fear p478

**7.50**    **False**

**7.51**    **False** – Elderly females.

**7.52**    **False** – They should be told.
Fear p447

**7.53**    **True**

**7.54**    **True**
A–Z p239

**7.55**    **Tru**
A–Z p8–12

**7.56**    **False** – It is approximately 50%.

**7.57**    **True** – It occurs in up to 30% of firefighters.
A–Z p260–3

**7.58**    **True**
A–Z p259

**7.59**    **True**

**7.60**    **True**

**7.61**    **True**

**7.62**    **False**

**7.63**    **True**
A–Z p58–60

**7.64**    **True**
A–Z p38–9

**7.65**    **False** – CAGE is a series of four questions about **C**ontrol of drinking, whether people are **A**nnoyed about your drinking, whether you feel **G**uilty about your drinking and whether you ever have an **E**ye-opener (an early morning drink).

**7.66**    **True** – It is a feature of most substance misuse.

**7.67**    **False**

**7.68**    **True**
A–Z p219

**7.69**    **True**
Fear p457

**7.70**    **True**

**7.71**    **False** – This was Freud's original view. It is now seen as an important source of information about the dynamic between patient and therapist and can be used to contribute to treatment.
A–Z p87

**7.72**    **False** – It is usually brief.

**7.73**    **True** – It occurs in over 70% of cases.

**7.74**    **True**

**7.75**    **True**

**7.76**    **False** – The risks are great and accurate diagnosis is of insufficient value to warrant brain biopsy.

**7.77**    **True**
A–Z p106–10

**7.78**    **True**

**7.79** **False** – The long-term prognosis is poor.
Fear p385

**7.80** **True**

**7.81** **True**

**7.82** **True**
A–Z p38–9

**7.83** **True**
A–Z p311

**7.84** **False** – Late winter and early spring births are more commonly affected, because of in utero exposure to viruses.

**7.85** **False** – It treats the movement disorder.
A–Z p167–9

**7.86** **True**
A–Z p171

**7.87** **True**

**7.88** **False** – Homozygosity is a risk factor.
A–Z p106–10, Fear p449

**7.89** **True**

**7.90** **True**

**7.91** **True**

**7.92** **False** – The reverse is true – confabulation is initially momentary and becomes fantastic as the condition progresses.

**7.93** **True**

**7.94** **True**

**7.95** **True**

**7.96** **True**

**7.97** **True**

**7.98** **True**

**7.99** **False** – They are seen over the iris.
A–Z p112–13

**7.100** **True**

**7.101** **False** – It is 0.4–0.6.

**7.102** **True**

**7.103** **False** – It is both a hallucinogen and a stimulant.

**7.104** **True**
A–Z p26–9

**7.105** **True**
A–Z p11

**7.106** **True**
A–Z p281–6

**7.107** **True**
A–Z p259

**7.108** **False** – It is subjectively identical.
A–Z p40

**7.109** **True**

**7.110** **False** – The gender incidence is equal.

**7.111** **False** – It is often severe.

**7.112** **True**

**7.113** **True**

**7.114** **True**

**7.115** **False** – They are more likely to be convicted, having been caught.

**7.116** **False**

**7.117** **False** – Smooth, soft skin.

**7.118** **False** – They are applicable in many other situations.

**7.119** **True**

**7.120** **False** – It is an indication for family therapy.

**7.121** **False** – Vaughn and Leff described expressed emotion as a risk factor for relapse in schizophrenia. Hooley and Teasdale described a highly critical spouse as a risk factor for relapse in depressive disorders.
A–Z p8–12

**7.122** **True**
A–Z p26–9

**7.123** **False**
A–Z p134

**7.124** **False** – The therapist takes the lead.

**7.125** **False** – The reverse is true.

**7.126** **True**

**7.127** **False** – Manic symptoms predominate.

**7.128** **False** – They occur in the first third of the night.

**7.129** **True**

**7.130**   **False** – Deaths caused by dangerous driving are far more prevalent.

**7.131**   **False** – Respiratory infection is the most common cause of death.

**7.132**   **True** – With a 30% prevalence rate.

**7.133**   **True**

**7.134**   **True**

**7.135**   **True**
        A–Z p21

**7.136**   **True**
        A–Z p169

**7.137**   **False** – Only alcohol dependence, not opiate dependence.
        A–Z p218–19

**7.138**   **True**

**7.139**   **True**

**7.140**   **False** – The quality of the therapeutic alliance between therapist and patient is the most critical factor.

**7.141**   **True**

**7.142**   **True** – This is its major effect.

**7.143**   **False** – It is a partial agonist.

**7.144**   **False** – β-Blockers may help.
        A–Z p19

**7.145**   **True** – It is psychogenic in this case.
        A–Z p45–6

**7.146**   **False** – It occurs during stages 3 and 4 (deep sleep).

**7.147** **False** – Only in 20%.
A–Z p258–9

**7.148** **False** – It is a feature of behaviourism and states that feelings and thoughts are not valid objects of scientific enquiry.
A–Z p58

**7.149** **False**

**7.150** **True**
Fear p453

**7.151** **True**

**7.152** **False** – IQ is usually unaffected.

**7.153** **True**
A–Z p167–9

**7.154** **True**
A–Z p202

**7.155** **True**
A–Z p26–9

**7.156** **False** – 4%.

**7.157** **True**

**7.158** **False** – They are either elementary or very complex and are often maintained for long periods.

**7.159** **True**

**7.160** **True**

**7.161** **True**

**7.162** **False** – This rarely occurs.

**7.163**  **False** – It is associated with Down's syndrome but is also seen in the general population.

**7.164**  **False** – It is recorded on Axis II.

**7.165**  **False** – It involves both individual and group therapy.

## EXTENDED MATCHING ITEMS

### 7.166 THEME: TREATMENT IN DRUG ADDICTION

1  **A** – Acamprosate
2  **I** – Naltrexone
3  **G** – Methadone

### 7.167 THEME: CLINICAL SYNDROMES

1  **B** – Capgras' syndrome
2  **C** – Cotard's syndrome
3  **D** – De Clerambault's syndrom
4  **J** – Turner's syndrome
   Fear p381–2

### 7.168 THEME: DIAGNOSIS

1  **D** – Friedreich's ataxia
2  **A** – Alzheimer's disease
3  **J** – Temporal lobe epilepsy
4  **F** – Gerstmann's syndrome
5  **E** – Ganser's syndrome

### 7.169 THEME: MOVEMENT DISORDER

1  **C** – Cogwheel rigidity
2  **G** – Myoclonic jerks
3  **D** – Epileptiform seizures
4  **H** – Tics

### 7.170 THEME: PREVENTION

1  **F & A** – Educating primary school children about the dangers of smoking and The Changing Minds Campaign led by the Royal College of Psychiatrists
2  **A & D** – Early intervention services for first-episode psychosis and Supportive psychotherapy to improve compliance with antipsychotics

3       **C & F** – Providing staffed hostel accommodation for recently discharged people with schizophrenia and The partners in Care Programme

**7.171   THEME: CULTURE-BOUND SYNDROMES**

1       **F** – Koro
2       **C** – Dhat
3       **G** – Latah
4       **I** – Piblokto
5       **J** – Windigo
6       **B** – Brain fag syndrome

**7.172   THEME: PROGNOSIS IN SCHIZOPHRENIA**

1       **G & H** – Older age at first onset and Rapid onset
2       **E & F** – Lower social class and Male gender
3       **D & I** – Keeping pets and Smoking more than 20 cigarettes daily

# PRACTICE PAPER 8

*Time allowed: 90 minutes*

## INDIVIDUAL STATEMENT QUESTIONS

**8.1** Perseveration is a feature of Noonan's syndrome.

**8.2** Post-traumatic stress disorder is common after childbirth.

**8.3** *Schnauzkrampf* is a movement disorder seen in schizophrenia.

**8.4** Approximate answers are associated with organic states.

**8.5** Narcolepsy involves increased rapid eye movement latency.

**8.6** Lewy bodies are seen in both Parkinson's disease and Lewy body dementia.

**8.7** Acamprosate is a γ-aminobutyric acid (GABA) analogue.

**8.8** Pregnancy is protective against the harmful effects of MDMA.

**8.9** Child sexual abuse has a negative correlation with eating disorders in later life.

**8.10** Night terrors are familial and continue until the late teens in most cases.

**8.11** Between 10 and 15% of prisoners have a diagnosis of secondary epilepsy as a result of head injury.

**8.12** Solvent abuse is more common in females than males.

**8.13** Korsakoff's syndrome is associated with significant frontal lobe dysfunction.

**8.14** A common presentation of Diogenes' syndrome is making an attempt to hide in barrel-shaped objects.

**8.15** Psychiatric patients on remand go home to await trial.

**8.16** Benzodiazepine withdrawal can cause depersonalisation.

**8.17** Replacement therapy may be useful in treatment of the excessive use of cocaine.

**8.18** Alcohol detoxification should be carried out in hospital for patients over 60 years of age because of the risk of serious complications in the community.

**8.19** Wernicke's encephalopathy can follow alcohol dependence, carbon monoxide poisoning, starvation or cerebrovascular accident.

**8.20** Female gender is an independent risk factor for suicide in the over-75 age group.

**8.21** The eldest child in a family is significantly more likely to become dependent on alcohol than younger children in the same family.

**8.22** The prognosis is poor in secondary encopresis.

**8.23** School refusal is synonymous with truancy.

**8.24** The EEG is abnormal in pseudodementia.

**8.25** Specific reading disorder has a positive association with soft neurological signs.

**8.26** Depression in the elderly presents with somatic complaints in inpatients but not in outpatients.

**8.27** Countertransference can enable a more effective engagement between therapist and patient.

**8.28** According to the 10th revision of the International Classification of Diseases (ICD-10), Lewy body dementia occurs most commonly in people over 65 years of age.

**8.29** The Hayflick limit relates to a robust boundary which should be established to manage aggression in learning difficulty.

**8.30** Learning difficulties are more prevalent in lower social classes.

**8.31** A single palmar crease is pathognomonic of Down's syndrome.

**8.32** The amyloid precursor protein gene is located on chromosome 19.

**8.33** People with bipolar disorder pose a greater risk to themselves than they pose to others.

**8.34** Cholinesterase inhibitors have an onset of action of 12–24 hours in mild-to-moderate Alzheimer's disease.

**8.35** Behaviourism suggests that classical conditioning is paramount and that operant conditioning can be disregarded.

**8.36** Alzheimer's disease is more common than vascular dementia.

**8.37** Motor neurone disease causes dysphasia.

**8.38** Self-discharge of patients with Munchausen's syndrome should be encouraged in most cases.

**8.39** Cognitive behavioural therapy aims for long-term personality change.

**8.40** Anorexia nervosa is associated with EEG changes.

**8.41** Homework is important in cognitive behavioural therapy.

**8.42** Transient depression can occur in manic states.

**8.43** Creutzfeldt–Jakob disease characteristically leads to cortical blindness and parietal lobe symptoms.

**8.44** As a means of suicide, drowning is more commonly seen in the elderly than the young.

**8.45** Akathisia is more commonly a source of complaint from relatives than from patients themselves, but is a risk factor for suicide in schizophrenia.

**8.46** Huntington's disease characteristically involves at least 145 CAG repeats.

**8.47** A cause is identified for the overwhelming majority of patients with mild learning difficulty.

**8.48** Male gender is associated with a good prognosis in schizophrenia.

**8.49** Windigo is characteristically seen in Asia.

**8.50** Panic attacks are associated with excess caffeine intake.

**8.51** Wilson's disease can lead to psychosis.

**8.52** Post-partum psychosis is characterised by insidious onset of gradually increasing psychosis.

**8.53** Schizophrenia is associated with perinatal complications.

**8.54** Patients with bulimia nervosa are generally more sexually experienced than patients with anorexia nervosa.

**8.55** There are almost 5,000,000 violent crimes every year in the United Kingdom.

**8.56** Pronominal reversal is a feature of infantile autism.

**8.57** There is a preference for routine and consistency in infantile autism.

**8.58** Fragile X syndrome is associated with brown eyes more often than by chance alone.

**8.59** Semantic dementia characteristically affects patients who are less than 65 years of age.

**8.60** There is evidence to suggest that motivational interviewing is of benefit in excessive use of alcohol.

**8.61** Individuals with post-traumatic stress disorder are at elevated risk of suicide if they experience combat-related guilt.

**8.62** Over 75% of people with alcohol dependence syndrome have a co-morbid psychiatric diagnosis.

**8.63** Friedreich's ataxia is progressive and involves hypertrophic obstructive cardiomyopathy and hyper-reflexia.

**8.64** Uninterrupted talking is generally of longer duration during telephone calls than during direct interpersonal exchanges.

**8.65** There is an association between postnatal depressive disorders and failure to bond with the child.

**8.66** Schizophreniform psychosis is seen in Wilson's disease.

**8.67** Solvent abuse in childhood correlates with low socioeconomic status.

**8.68** Bipolar affective disorder often presents after childbirth.

**8.69** Waxy flexibility is commonly associated with frontal lobe tumours.

**8.70** Relatives of patients with Gilles de la Tourette's syndrome have increased rates of obsessions and compulsions compared with the general population.

**8.71** Chronic fatigue syndrome is associated with greater social morbidity than chronic juvenile arthritis when it occurs in children.

**8.72** Peer approval is a characteristic feature of attention deficit hyperactivity disorder (ADHD) in school-age children.

**8.73** In school refusal, young age at first instance is a good prognostic indicator.

**8.74** The mirror sign is positive in severe Alzheimer's disease.

**8.75** Deficits associated with Lewy body dementia include impaired visuo-spatial ability and impaired frontal subcortical skills.

**8.76** Rotational dizziness is a symptom of severe anxiety.

**8.77** Schizophrenia-like psychosis in epilepsy can be distinguished from schizophrenia because there is often a warm affect and visual hallucinations have a mystical content.

**8.78** Postnatal blues typically peak 3–4 days postpartum.

**8.79** Attention deficit hyperactivity disorder (ADHD) may respond to treatment with clonidine.

**8.80** A subjective sense of constriction is characteristic of anxiety.

**8.81** Benzodiazepine use can cause ataxia.

**8.82** Sublimation can result in positive outcomes from initially negative emotions.

**8.83** You are more likely to be injured by someone with schizophrenia than by a police car in the United Kingdom.

**8.84** Klinefelter's syndrome is strongly associated with interpersonal violence when intoxicated.

**8.85** Deliberate self-harm in people with learning difficulty is most problematic between the ages of 10 and 30 years.

**8.86** Cognitive behavioural therapy is the treatment of choice in social phobia.

**8.87**    Cortisol levels are increased in anorexia nervosa.

**8.88**    Gender dysphoric disorder is associated with homosexuality.

**8.89**    The long-term prognosis of enuresis is poor.

**8.90**    Wernicke's encephalopathy is an alcohol-related problem which occurs in clear consciousness.

**8.91**    Cotard's syndrome can occur in depressive disorders and Alzheimer's disease, but not in schizophrenia.

**8.92**    Cognitive errors in depression include arbitrary inference and dichotomous abstraction.

**8.93**    Catatonia is a common presentation of schizophrenia.

**8.94**    The median survival after diagnosis of Alzheimer's disease is 10 years.

**8.95**    Faecal soiling is more common than night-time bedwetting in 4-year-olds.

**8.96**    The third revision of the Millon Clinical Multiaxial Inventory (MCMI-III) is validated for use in the general population.

**8.97**    Current drug and alcohol use renders a patient completely unsuitable for psychodynamic psychotherapy.

**8.98**    The overall weight of the brain is normal in Down's syndrome.

**8.99**    Systemic therapy uses circular questioning, which has a dual role of gathering information from the family and introducing information to them.

**8.100**    90% of people with obsessive-compulsive disorder have motor compulsions.

**8.101**    A history of depressive disorder is a risk factor for Alzheimer's disease.

**8.102** The most common cause of death in infants is accidental death.

**8.103** Delusional perception is commonly preceded by delusional atmosphere.

**8.104** Arson may be committed so that the perpetrator can rescue people from the fire.

**8.105** Couvade syndrome is a hysterical disorder.

**8.106** Prevalence rates of child sexual offending are accurate and well established.

**8.107** Down's syndrome is associated with hypertonia.

**8.108** Non-specific random theta and delta activity is seen in normal pressure hydrocephalus.

**8.109** Fear of losing control of eating is seen in anorexia nervosa.

**8.110** Subacute sclerosing panencephalitis usually presents 6–9 months after the original infection with cognitive decline and myoclonus.

**8.111** Symptoms are left-sided in most hypochondriacal patients.

**8.112** Autoscopy is a common feature of near-death experiences.

**8.113** Elderly patients with delusional disorder can only be treated safely in hospital, because of the risk of electrocution.

**8.114** Severe depressive disorder with psychotic symptoms is a risk factor for Alzheimer's disease.

**8.115** Motivational interviewing uses the 'stages of change model' proposed by Prochaska and di Maggio.

**8.116** A cup of coffee characteristically contains 600 mg of caffeine.

**8.117** In the absence of any co-morbid problems, the prognosis of elective mutism is poor.

**8.118** Elective mutism, when present, characteristically occurs within the home.

**8.119** The heritability of conduct disorder is 0.7–0.9.

**8.120** Refusal to plead leads to unfitness to plead.

**8.121** Arsonists rarely escape unpunished because the crime is so serious.

**8.122** Angelman's syndrome involves a low threshold for laughing.

**8.123** Laurence–Moon–Biedl syndrome is associated with obesity.

**8.124** Risperidone is often helpful in treatment of attention deficit hyperactivity disorder (ADHD) in childhood.

**8.125** Gestalt therapy involves reviewing a person's achievements during their life.

**8.126** Acamprosate is a glutamate agonist.

**8.127** Edward's syndrome is more common in males.

**8.128** Temporal arteritis often presents as depression in the elderly.

**8.129** Median survival from diagnosis is longer in vascular dementia than in Alzheimer's disease.

**8.130** Fear of the dark is seen in Wernicke's encephalopathy.

**8.131** Tic disorders usually have a chronic, remitting and relapsing course over many years.

**8.132** Munchausen's syndrome is more prevalent in females.

**8.133** Cluster B personality disorders include narcissistic and paranoid.

**8.134** Munchausen's syndrome presents with physical rather than psychiatric complaints.

**8.135** Disturbance of affect is pronounced in hebephrenic schizophrenia.

**8.136** The peak age of offending in the United Kingdom is younger in females than in males.

**8.137** Morbid jealousy has a strong association with minor violent crime.

**8.138** Male gender is a good prognostic indicator in anorexia nervosa.

**8.139** Cannabis use is associated with a relative risk of 2.5 for schizophrenia.

**8.140** Babies should sleep on their front as this is more comfortable.

**8.141** Non-organic enuresis is determined almost exclusively by social factors.

**8.142** Compulsions increase anxiety in obsessive-compulsive disorder.

**8.143** Secondary depression is more common in females than males.

**8.144** Influenza causes difficulties for the fetus in utero, despite being unable to cross the placenta.

**8.145** Huntington's disease characteristically has an earlier age of onset if the father is the diseased parent.

**8.146** Incidence of late paraphrenia in elderly populations is approximately 200 per 100, 000 per year.

**8.147** Selective punishment involves the use of aversive events to decrease maladaptive behaviour.

**8.148** Somatisation is more common in depressive disorder in adolescents compared with adults.

**8.149** Alcohol ingestion can cause severe and acute symptoms in conjunction with metronidazole.

**8.149** Alcohol ingestion can cause severe and acute symptoms in conjunction with metronidazole.

**8.150** Most cases of post-partum psychosis have a good prognosis.

**8.151** Perceptual abnormalities are more suggestive of delirium than of dementia.

**8.152** Simple tics are most common in girls and occur at a mean age of onset of 7 years.

**8.153** Children who are physically abused by their parents do not form an attachment to them.

**8.154** Monozygotic concordance rates for schizophrenia are 45%.

**8.155** According to the 10th revision of the International Classification of Diseases (ICD-10), severe mental retardation features an IQ of 24–39.

**8.156** Autistic disorder is associated with the refrigerator mother.

**8.157** Socratic questioning is useful in psychoanalytic psychotherapy.

**8.158** Possession states are usually dissociative.

**8.159** Tangentiality does not discriminate between mania and schizophrenia.

**8.160** Cognitive analytic therapy is suitable for use in the elderly, but only after substantial adaptation.

**8.161** People with dementia always lack capacity to consent to surgery.

**8.162** Disulfiram-like effects are seen following administration of high doses of penicillin.

**8.163** Temper tantrums in early childhood are associated with conduct disorder in later childhood.

**8.164** Mothers can reinforce attachment behaviour by crying.

**8.165** Most normal homicides are committed by males.

# EXTENDED MATCHING QUESTIONS

### 8.166 THEME: PSYCHOTROPIC EFFECTS OF ILLICIT SUBSTANCES

| | |
|---|---|
| A | Amphetamines |
| B | Amyl nitrate |
| C | Barbiturates |
| D | Benzodiazepines |
| E | Cannabis |
| F | Crack cocaine |
| G | Heroin |
| H | LSD (lysergic acid diethylamide) |
| I | Solvents |
| J | Steroids |

**Choose the illicit substance from the list above most closely associated with each of the following effects.**

1      A sense of relaxation and revelation associated with dreaminess and, later, hunger.

2      A sense of exhilaration, increased confidence and potency, with suppression of appetite which is of rapid onset over minutes and brief duration lasting less than an hour.

3      Gradual onset over an hour, with initial excitement followed by visual hallucinations and emotional disturbance lasting for several hours.

4      Drowsiness and contentment, associated with powerful analgesic effects.

## 8.167 THEME: PSYCHIATRIC DISORDERS ASSOCIATED WITH LEARNING DISABILITY SYNDROMES

| | |
|---|---|
| A | Aicardi's syndrome |
| B | Cornelia de Lange's syndrome |
| C | Fetal alcohol syndrome |
| D | Lesch–Nyhan syndrome |
| E | Noonan's syndrome |
| F | Phenylketonuria |
| G | Prader–Willi syndrome |
| H | Smith–Magenis syndrome |
| I | Velocardiofacial syndrome |
| J | Williams' syndrome |

**Which syndrome from the list above is most closely associated with the following psychiatric presentations?**

1    Disinhibited behaviour characterised by aggression and hyperkinetic disorders. Affective change is prominent.
2    Significantly increased risk of schizophrenia, affective disorders and autistic spectrum disorder.
3    Lethargy, self-injurious and aggressive behaviour and marked sleep disturbance.

## 8.168   THEME: MOVEMENT DISORDERS

| | |
|---|---|
| A | Acute dystonia |
| B | Akathisia |
| C | Clopixol |
| D | Clozapine |
| E | Hyoscine |
| F | Negativism |
| G | Procyclidine |
| H | Propranolol |
| I | Schnauzkrampf |
| J | Tardive dyskinesia |

**Choose the most likely diagnosis (A–E) and most appropriate intervention (F–J) from the list above for each of the following presentations:**

1   A 24-year-old man has recently started his first antipsychotic and finds his legs difficult to keep still.

2   A 56-year-old woman has suffered with schizophrenia for many years and has been poorly controlled on several antipsychotics. She develops choreoathetoid movements of the face after 4 years on her current antipsychotic and attributes this to black magic and the internet.

3   A 19-year-old man develops an acutely stiff neck and difficulty swallowing several days after having 3 doses of intramuscular haloperidol during his first episode of psychosis.

## 8.169    THEME: GRIEF REACTIONS

| | |
|---|---|
| A | A feeling of numbness |
| B | Ability to enjoy memories of good times |
| C | Anhedonia |
| D | Guilt about past actions |
| E | Loss of sense of purpose |
| F | Resolution of symptoms |
| G | Shock |
| H | Suicidal thoughts |
| I | Weeping |
| J | Weight loss |

**Choose two symptoms from the list above which relate to the following:**

1    The first stage of a normal grief reaction.
2    The third (final) stage of a normal grief reaction.
3    Features which are not seen as part of a normal grief reaction.

## 8.170  THEME: PSYCHIATRIC RATING SCALES

| | |
|---|---|
| A | Beck Depression Inventory (BDI) |
| B | Composite International Diagnostic Interview (CID |
| C | Global Assessment of Function (GAF)I)N |
| D | Hamilton Depression Scale (HAM-D) |
| E | HCR-20 |
| F | Hospital Anxiety and Depression Scale (HADS) |
| G | Liebowitz |
| H | Present State Examination |
| I | Structured Clinical Interview for Diagnosis (SCID) |
| J | Structured Clinical Interview for Diagnosis-II (SCID-II) |

**Choose the scale from the list above which is best described by each of the following:**

1   A clinician-rated scale predicting risk of interpersonal violence.
2   Clinician-rated scale, the results of which are used by a computer program known as CATEGO to produce a diagnosis.
3   Clinician-rated scale used to assess function on Axis V of the 4th revision of the Diagnostic and Statistical Manual of Mental Disorders (DSM-IV).
4   Clinician-rated scale examining depressive symptoms.

## 8.171 THEME: HAEMATOLOGICAL INVESTIGATIONS

| | |
|---|---|
| A | A neutrophil count of 0.4 X 10⁹/litre |
| B | A neutrophil count of of 4.2 X 10⁹/litre |
| C | Lithium assay of 0.2 mmol/litre |
| D | Lithium assay of 0.7 mmol/litre |
| E | Lithium assay of 2.3 mmol/litre |
| F | Plasma alanine aminotransferase of 30 IU/litre |
| G | Plasma bilirubin of 16 mmol/litre |
| H | Plasma γ-glutamyl transpeptidase of 43 IU/litre |
| I | Plasma γ-glutamyl transpeptidase of 93 IU/litre |
| J | Plasma osmolality of 301 mosmol/kg |

**Select the haematological value from the list above which most supports the following clinical scenarios.**

1    Regular and excessive consumption of alcohol.
2    A result indicating that clozapine should be stopped immediately.
3    Appropriate dosage of lithium.

## 8.172 THEME: NHS STRUCTURES AND INITIATIVES

| | |
|---|---|
| A | Annual Delivery Plan |
| B | Assertive Outreach Teams |
| C | Changing Minds |
| D | Clinical Governance |
| E | Controls Assurance |
| F | Early Intervention Service |
| G | Home Treatment Teams |
| H | Partners in Care |
| I | Primary-Care Trusts |
| J | The NHS Plan |

**Choose the most appropriate term from the list above for each of the following:**

1    The framework which monitors the NHS to ensure that services are of sufficiently high and ever-improving standards.

2    Local healthcare delivery services which aim to deliver a high standard of care to outpatients with severe and enduring mental health problems who are also difficult to engage.

3    A programme devised by central government to modernise and improve healthcare services nationwide over 10 years.

4    A campaign mounted by the Royal College of Psychiatrists to empower carers of patients with mental illness to work more effectively alongside healthcare professionals.

# PRACTICE PAPER 8

## Answers

### INDIVIDUAL STATEMENT QUESTIONS

**8.1**  **True**

**8.2**  **False**
A–Z p260–3

**8.3**  **True** – It is a form of involuntary grimacing.

**8.4**  **True** – Also with hysteria and Ganser's syndrome.

**8.5**  **False** – The rapid eye movement latency is decreased.

**8.6**  **True**

**8.7**  **True**
Fear p483

**8.8**  **False** – Illicit substances are likely to be particularly harmful in pregnancy.

**8.9**  **False** – There is a positive correlation.

**8.10**  **False** – They usually begin and end in childhood.

**8.11**  **False** – The prevalence of epilepsy in prisoners is similar to that seen in matched controls.

**8.12**  **False** – The sex incidence is equal.

**8.13**  **True**
A–Z p345–6

**8.14**  **False**

**8.15**  **False** – They may be remanded on bail (to go into the community) or into custody (to go to prison).

**8.16**  **True**
A–Z p58–60

**8.17**  **False**

**8.18**  **False** – Inpatient detoxification should be carried out for patients with complications, and patients with existing medical problems, or when detoxification in the community would fail for other reasons.

**8.19**  **True** – Also hyperemesis, gastrointestinal tract lesions and medial temporal lobe lesions.

**8.20**  **False** – Male gender is a risk factor.

**8.21**  **False**

**8.22**  **False** – It is good.

**8.23**  **False**

**8.24**  **False**

**8.25**  **True**

**8.26**  **False** – It does so in both groups.
A–Z p11

**8.27**  **True**

**8.28**  **False** – Lewy body dementia does not feature in 10th revision of the International Classification of Diseases (ICD-10).

**8.29**  **False** – It refers to the fact that cells will not divide for ever. It has been suggested as a factor in the limited lifespan achievable by living organisms.

**8.30**  **True**

**8.31**  **False** – It is a non-specific sign seen in normal populations.

**8.32**  **False** – It is located on chromosome 21 and this explains why people with Down's syndrome have a higher incidence of Alzheimer's disease at a younger age.
A–Z p106–10, Fear p449

**8.33**  **True** – Almost 20% will commit suicide.

**8.34**  **False** – The onset of action is 4–6 weeks.
Fear p465

**8.35**  **False** – It values both.

**8.36**  **True**

**8.37**  **False** – It causes dysphagia but not dysphasia.
A–Z p218

**8.38**  **True**
A–Z p218–19

**8.39**  **False** – It aims to palliate symptoms.

**8.40**  **True** – These result from metabolic encephalopathy.
A–Z p26–9

**8.41**  **True**

**8.42**  **True** – The mood is generally fluctuant.

**8.43**  **True**
A–Z p110–11

**8.44**  **True**
A–Z p310–11

**8.45**  **True**
A–Z p19

**8.46**   **False** – It involves 45.
A–Z p167–9

**8.47**   **False** – No specific cause is found in most cases.

**8.48**   **False** – This indicates a poorer prognosis than female gender.
A–Z p281–6

**8.49**   **False** – It was described in North America.

**8.50**   **True**
A–Z p69

**8.51**   **True**
A–Z p112–13

**8.52**   **False** – Onset is abrupt and the psychosis fluctuates.

**8.53**   **True**

**8.54**   **True**
A–Z p26–9

**8.55**   **False** – There are 500,000.
Fear p425

**8.56**   **True**
A–Z p53

**8.57**   **True**
A–Z p53

**8.58**   **False** – Blue eyes.

**8.59**   **True**
Fear p454

**8.60**   **True**

**8.61**   **True**
A–Z p310–11

**8.62**   **False** – Approximately 50%.
A–Z p20

**8.63**   **False** – It involves hyporeflexia.

**8.64**   **True**

**8.65**   **True**

**8.66**   **True**

**8.67**   **True**

**8.68**   **True**
A–Z p8–12

**8.69**   **True**

**8.70**   **True**

**8.71**   **True**

**8.72**   **False** – Peer rejection is common.

**8.73**   **True**

**8.74**   **True**
A–Z p106–10

**8.75**   **True** – There are also marked impairments in concentration.
A–Z p97–8

**8.76**   **False** – Dizziness is a symptom, but not rotational dizziness.
A–Z p38–9

**8.77**   **True**
A–Z p136–7

**8.78**   **True**
A–Z p259

**8.79**    **True**

**8.80**    **False**
A–Z p38–9

**8.81**    **True**

**8.82**    **True**

**8.83**    **False** – The rates are similar.

**8.84**    **False** – There is no such link.

**8.85**    **True**

**8.86**    **True**

**8.87**    **True**
A–Z p26–9

**8.88**    **False**

**8.89**    **False** – The long-term prognosis is very good.

**8.90**    **False** – It occurs with clouding of consciousness.

**8.91**    **False** – It is seen in schizophrenia.

**8.92**    **False** – Arbitrary inference, dichotomous thinking and
selective abstraction, amongst others.
A–Z p12–14

**8.93**    **False**

**8.94**    **False** – 6 years.
Fear p448

**8.95**    **False**

**8.96**    **False**

**8.97**     **False** – But it makes them much less suitable.
Fear p517

**8.98**     **False** – It is reduced by up to 20%.

**8.99**     **True**

**8.100**    **False** – 50–60%.
A–Z p38–9

**8.101**    **True**

**8.102**    **False** – It is sudden infant death.

**8.103**    **True**
A–Z p243

**8.104**    **True** – This is seen in 'hero fire setters'.

**8.105**    **True**

**8.106**    **False** – They are difficult to be accurate about.

**8.107**    **False** – It is associated with hypotonia.

**8.108**    **True**
A–Z p169

**8.109**    **True**
A–Z p26–9

**8.110**    **False** – It usually presents 2–12 years after the initial measles
infection.
A–Z p134

**8.111**    **True**
A–Z p171

**8.112**    **True**

**8.113**    **False**

**8.114** **True**

**8.115** **False** – Prochaska and di Clemente

**8.116** **False** – 80–160 mg

**8.117** **True**

**8.118** **False** – It occurs most often at school.

**8.119** **False** – It is 0.4–0.6.

**8.120** **False** – To be unfit to plead you must be unable to plead.

**8.121** **False** – Most cases of arson are never prosecuted.

**8.122** **True**

**8.123** **True**
Fear p384

**8.124** **False**

**8.125** **False** – It focuses on the current situation.

**8.126** **False** – It is an antagonist.

**8.127** **False** – It is more common in females.

**8.128** **True**
Fear p457

**8.129** **True**

**8.130** **True**
A–Z p343–5

**8.131** **False** – They usually resolve after a few years and do not recur.

**8.132** **False** – The reverse is true.
A–Z p218–19

**8.133** **False** – Antisocial, borderline, histrionic and narcissistic are in cluster B. Paranoid personality disorder is cluster A.
A–Z p115

**8.134** **False** – It can present with either.

**8.135** **True**

**8.136** **True**

**8.137** **False** – It is strongly associated with serious violent crime, especially homicide.

**8.138** **True**

**8.139** **True**

**8.140** **False** – There is an association between an increased risk of sudden infant death syndrome and babies sleeping on their front.

**8.141** **False** – 70% of subjects have a relative with continence problems.

**8.142** **False** – They reduce anxiety.

**8.143** **False** – It has equal sex incidence.

**8.144** **True**

**8.145** **False** – The age of onset is earlier if the mother is the diseased parent.
A–Z p167–9

**8.146** **False** – It is 20 per 100,000 per year.

**8.147** **True** – It is used in operant therapy.
A–Z p320–1

**8.148** **True**

**8.149** **True**

**8.150** **True**

**8.151** **True**

**8.152** **False** – They are more common in boys.

**8.153** **False** – They form attachments but they are rarely securely attached.

**8.154** **True** – Dizygotic concordance is 10%.
A–Z p287–91

**8.155** **False** – It involves an IQ of 20–34.

**8.156** **True** – Although this theory is now discounted.

**8.157** **False** – It is used in cognitive therapy.

**8.158** **True**
A–Z p259

**8.159** **True**

**8.160** **False** – It is suitable for use in the elderly with little modification.
Fear p466

**8.161** **False**

**8.162** **False** – Metronidazole causes a similar adverse reaction to even small amounts of alcohol.

**8.163** **True**

**8.164** **True** – Also by smiling and moving.
A–Z p46–7

**8.165** **True** – Females commit a very small proportion of total homicides.

# EXTENDED MATCHING QUESTIONS

### 8.166 THEME: PSYCHOTROPIC EFFECTS OF ILLICIT SUBSTANCES

1    **E** – Cannabis
2    **F** – Crack cocaine
3    **H** – LSD
4    **G** – Heroin

### 8.167 THEME: PSYCHIATRIC DISORDERS ASSOCIATED WITH LEARNING DISABILITY SYNDROMES

1    **C** – Fetal alcohol syndrome
2    **I** – Velocardiofacial syndrome
3    **A** – Aicardi syndrome
      Fear p394

### 8.168 THEME: MOVEMENT DISORDERS

1    **B & H** – Akathisia and Propranolol
2    **D & J** – Clozapine Tardive and dyskinesia
3    **A & G** – Acute dystonia and Procyclidine

### 8.169 THEME: GRIEF REACTIONS

1    **A & G** – A feeling of numbness and shock
2    **B & F** – Ability to enjoy memories of good times and
      Resolution of symptoms
3    **D & H** – Guilt about past actions and suicidal thoughts.
      The other symptoms all occur in the second stage of
      a normal grief reaction.
      A–Z p154–5

## 8.170 THEME: PSYCHIATRIC RATING SCALES

1    **E** – HCR-20. HCR stands for **H**istorical, **C**linical and **R**isk management.
2    **H** – Present State Examination
3    **C** – Global Assessment of Function (GAF)
4    **D** – Hamilton Depression Scale (HAM-D)
     Fear p275–6

## 8.171 THEME: HAEMATOLOGICAL INVESTIGATIONS

1    **I** – Plasma γ-glutamyl transpeptidase of 93 IU/litre
2    **A** – A neutrophil count of 0.4 $\times 10^9$/litre
3    **D** – Lithium assay of 0.7 mmol/litre

## 8.172 THEME: NHS STRUCTURES AND INITATIVES

1    **D** – Clinical Governance
2    **B** – Assertive Outreach Teams
3    **I** – The NHS Plan
4    **E** – Partner in Care

# INDEX